THE 2001 ANNUAL: Volume 1 Training

(The Thirty-Sixth Annual)

JOSSEY-BASS/PFEIFFER
A Wiley Company
San Francisco

THE
2001 ANNUAL:
Volume 1
Training

(The Thirty-Sixth Annual)

Edited by Elaine Biech

JOSSEY-BASS/PFEIFFER
A Wiley Company
San Francisco

Published by
JOSSEY-BASS/PFEIFFER
A Wiley Company
350 Sansome Street, 5th Floor
San Francisco, California 94104-1342
(415) 433-1740; Fax (415) 433-0499
(800) 274-4434; Fax (800) 569-0443

www.pfeiffer.com

Acquiring Editor: Matthew Holt
Director of Development: Kathleen Dolan Davies
Developmental Editors: Rebecca Taff and Susan Rachmeler
Senior Production Editor: Dawn Kilgore
Manufacturing Manager: Becky Carreño

Printing 10 9 8 7 6 5 4 3 2 1

PREFACE

2001! Welcome to the official start of the new century. And welcome to the thirtieth year of publication for the *Annuals*. Thirty years! What were you doing in 1971? Starting your first job? Attending high school? Grade school? Perhaps you had not been born yet? Our time-obsessed culture seldom allows us the opportunity to reflect on where we were when, nor the time to think, plan, or dream about our future. What's in store for you? And what's in store for the training and consulting professional?

Recent publications have attempted to give us a peek at the future. Some of their predictions are continuations of those we have heard before. Others may become important new influences in the next few years. What current trends will continue to influence the human resource profession?

- The speed of change will continue to increase.
- Collaboration will continue to be the way business is conducted.
- Clients, internal and external, will continue to expect turnkey delivery of services.
- Outsourcing will continue to grow.
- Technology will continue to be more powerful, more important, and more versatile.

What's new that might affect the human resource profession in the future?

- Simulation, used in the Department of Defense for years, may be a new tool for trainers.
- Learning will not be a separate event, but integrated into daily life—every day.
- E-books may replace the familiar hardcover, paperback, and even the training staple: three-ring binders.
- Interchangeable e-learning modules may be customized to each learner's needs.
- Net connections, cell phones, and other electronic tools may be built into your clothing.

This year's *Annual* is sure to help you with the increasing speed of change, because it contains many tools to help with your training and consulting tasks. Submissions in the technology areas will help you and your clients stay on top of knowledge management and e-learning. Other submissions address topics such as generation X, coaching leaders, achieving balance, organizational values, and many others that will make your job easier. So sit back, peruse the *Annual,* and think about how you might use the content to support what you will be doing this coming year.

The *Annual* series is provided in two volumes for you: Volume 1, Training, and Volume 2, Consulting. The Training volume focuses on skill building and knowledge enhancement, as well as on professional development for trainers. The Consulting volume focuses on intervention techniques and organizational systems, as well as on professional development for consultants. The performance-improvement technologist, whose role is one of combined trainer and consultant, will find valuable resources in both volumes. Both cover some of the same topics, such as "teamwork," but present the activities, instruments, and articles from the perspective of a trainer or a consultant.

For example, if you are looking for a workshop activity that teaches the skills required to be a good team member, turn to the Training volume. On the other hand, if you are looking for an intervention technique to increase the performance of an intact team, turn to the Consulting volume. For example, this year Edward Hampton presents a training activity for understanding the value of taking risks in teams, which you will find in the Training volume. Lynn Baker presents an activity that helps a team appreciate how it could be more effective in making decisions, which is in the Consulting volume. Both of these activities are located under the "Team" category. And yes, all activities in each volume may be adapted and used for either purpose by any astute human resource professional. This doubles their value for you.

The *Annual* series has been valuable to the training and consulting professions for the past thirty years for many reasons. First, and most importantly, the *Annuals* provide a variety of materials that cover many topics, from the basics to cutting-edge issues. The focus is on what you as a trainer or consultant require in order to improve your own competencies in areas such as facilitation skills, team building, consultation techniques, and opening and closing techniques. The *Annuals* also provide information for you to use to design materials or to develop strategy for your internal or external clients. Second, the *Annuals* are valuable because the materials provide several formats. You will find instruments for individuals, teams, and organizations; experiential learning activities to round out workshops, team building, or consulting assignments; and articles to assign as pre-reading, to read to increase your own knowledge base, or to use as reference materials for your writing or design tasks. Third, the *Annuals* are ready when you are. All of the materials may be duplicated for educational and training purposes. If you want to adapt or modify the materials to tailor them for your audience's needs, go right ahead. We request only that the credit statement found on the copyright page be included on all copies. In addition, if you intend to reproduce the materials in publications for sale or if you wish to use the materials on a large-scale basis (more than one hundred copies in one year), please contact us for written permission. Our liberal copyright policy makes it easy and fast for you to use the materials to do your job. Please call us if you have any questions.

Although the *2001 Annuals* are the newest in the series, you will benefit from having the entire series for your use. They are available in paperback or as a three-ring notebook; most volumes are also available on an easy-to-transport CD-ROM (as the *Pfeiffer & Company Library*). Why not check it out?

The *Annuals* have always been a valuable resource for the profession. The key is that the materials come from professionals like you—trainers, consultants, facilitators, educators, and performance-improvement technologists. This ensures that the materials have been tried and perfected in real-life settings to meet real-world needs. To this end, we encourage you to submit materials to be considered for publication in the *Annual*. At your request, we will provide a copy of the guidelines for preparing your materials.

We are interested in receiving experiential learning activities (group learning activities based on the five stages of the experiential learning cycle: experiencing, publishing, processing, generalizing, and applying); inventories, questionnaires, and surveys (both paper-and-pencil as well as electronic rating scales); and presentation and discussion resources (articles that may include theory related to practical application). Contact the Jossey-Bass/Pfeiffer Editorial Department at the address listed on the copyright page for copies of our guidelines for contributors or contact me directly at Box 657, Portage, WI 53901; on e-mail at Elaine@ebbweb.com; or call our office at 608-742-5005. We welcome your comments, ideas, and contributions.

Thanks go to the dedicated people at Jossey-Bass/Pfeiffer who produced the *2001 Annuals:* Kathleen Dolan Davies, Matthew Holt, Ocean Howell, Dawn Kilgore, Susan Rachmeler, and Rebecca Taff. Thanks also to Beth Drake of ebb associates inc, who organized this huge task and ensured that all the deadlines were met.

Most importantly, thank you to our authors, who have once again shared your ideas, techniques, and materials so that the rest of us may benefit. Thank you on behalf of all training and consulting professionals everywhere.

Elaine Biech
Editor
August 2000

About Jossey-Bass/Pfeiffer

Jossey-Bass/Pfeiffer is actively engaged in publishing insightful human resource development (HRD) materials. The organization has earned an international reputation as the leading source of practical resources that are immediately useful to today's consultants, trainers, facilitators, and managers in a variety of industries. All materials are designed by practicing professionals who are continually experimenting with new techniques. Thus, readers and users benefit from the fresh and thoughtful approach that underlies Jossey-Bass/Pfeiffer's experientially based materials, books, workbooks, instruments, and other learning resources and programs. This broad range of products is designed to help human resource practitioners increase individual, group, and organizational effectiveness and provide a variety of training and intervention technologies, as well as background in the field.

CONTENTS

---

*See Experiential Learning Activities Categories, p. 6, for an explanation of the numbering system.

**Topic is "cutting edge."

General Introduction
to the 2001 Annual, Training

The 2001 Annual: Volume 1, Training is the thirty-sixth volume in the *Annual* series, a collection of practical and useful materials for professionals in the broad area described as human resource development (HRD). The materials are written by and for professionals, including trainers, organization-development and organization-effectiveness consultants, performance-improvement technologists, educators, instructional designers, and others.

Each *Annual* has three main sections: *experiential learning activities; inventories, questionnaires, and surveys;* and *presentation and discussion resources.* Each published submission is classified in one of the following categories: Individual Development, Communication, Problem Solving, Groups, Teams, Consulting and Facilitating, Leadership, and Organizations. Within each category, pieces are further classified into logical subcategories, which are identified in the introductions to the three sections.

This year we have added a new subcategory to the "Organizations" category, which first appeared in the 1999 *Annual.* "Vision, Mission, Values, Strategy" joins "Communication" as the second subcategory in "Organizations." Although these topics have been addressed in the past, it may have been difficult to locate them in the former structure. Appropriate past submissions will be cross-referenced during the next update to the *Reference Guide to Handbooks and Annuals,* which indexes all the materials by key words.

A new subcategory, "Technology," was added in the 1999 *Annual.* Much has changed for the HRD professional in recent years, and technology has lead much of that change. Given the important role technology plays, we will continue to publish material that relates technology to the HRD field and explains how the HRD professional can use technology as a tool.

We continue to identify "cutting edge" topics in this *Annual.* This designation highlights topics that present information, concepts, tools, or perspectives that may be recent additions to the profession or that have not previously appeared in the *Annual.*

The series continues to provide an opportunity for HRD professionals who wish to share their experiences, their viewpoints, and their processes with their colleagues. To that end, Jossey-Bass/Pfeiffer publishes guidelines for potential authors. These guidelines are available from the Pfeiffer editorial department at Jossey-Bass, Inc., A Wiley Company, in San Francisco, California.

Materials are selected for the *Annuals* based on the quality of the ideas, applicability to real-world concerns, relevance to current HRD issues, clarity of presentation, and ability to enhance our readers' professional development. In addition, we choose experiential learning activities that will create a high degree of enthusiasm among the participants and add enjoyment to the learning process. As in the past several years, the contents of each *Annual* span a wide range of subject matter, reflecting the range of interests of our readers.

Our contributor list includes a wide selection of experts in the field: in-house practitioners, consultants, and academically based professionals. A list of contributors to this *Annual* can be found at the end of the volume, including their names, affiliations, addresses, telephone numbers, facsimile numbers, and e-mail addresses. Readers will find this list useful if they wish to locate the authors of specific pieces for feedback, comments, or questions. Further information is presented in a brief biographical sketch of each contributor that appears at the conclusion of each article. We publish this information to encourage "networking," which continues to be a valuable mainstay in the field of human resource development.

We are pleased with the high quality of material that is submitted for publication each year and often regret that we have page limitations. In addition, just as we cannot publish every manuscript we receive, you may find that not all published works are equally useful to you. Therefore, we encourage and invite ideas, materials, and suggestions that will help us to make subsequent *Annuals* as useful as possible to all of our readers.

Introduction
to the Experiential Learning Activities Section

Experiential learning activities ensure that lasting learning occurs. They should be selected with a specific learning objective in mind. These objectives are based on the participants' needs and the facilitator's skills. Although the experiential learning activities presented here all vary in goals, group size, time required and process,[1] they all incorporate one important element: questions that ensure learning has occurred. This discussion, led by the facilitator, assists participants to process the activity, to internalize the learning, and to relate it to their day-to-day situations. It is this element that creates the unique experience and learning opportunity that only an experiential learning activity can bring to the group process.

Readers have used the *Annuals'* experiential learning activities for years to enhance their training and consulting events. Each learning experience is complete and includes all lecturettes, handout content, and other written material necessary to facilitate the activity. In addition many include variations of the design that the facilitator might find useful. If the activity does not fit perfectly with your objective, within your time frame, or to your group size, we encourage you to adapt the activity by adding your own variations. You will find additional experiential learning activities listed in the "Experiential Learning Activities Categories" chart that immediately follows this introduction.

The 2001 Annual: Volume 1, Training includes thirteen activities, in the following categories:

Individual Development: Sensory Awareness

670. Spirituality at Work: Aiding Personal Growth and Development, by Steven L. Phillips and Christina L. Collins

---

[1]It would be redundant to print here a caveat for the use of experiential learning activities, but HRD professionals who are not experienced in the use of this training technology are strongly urged to read the "Introduction" to the *Reference Guide to Handbooks and Annuals* (1999 Edition). This article presents the theory behind the experiential-learning cycle and explains the necessity of adequately completing each phase of the cycle to allow effective learning to occur.

Individual Development: Life-Career Planning

671. What Works Best? Identifying Learning Styles, by Lois B. Hart

672. Passion and Purpose: Helping Employees Realign with the Organization, by Patricia Boverie and Michael Kroth

Communication: Conflict

673. Workplace Scenarios: Dealing with Emotional Behavior, by Robert William Lucas

Communication: Feedback

674. I Appreciate: Giving Affirmations, by A. Carol Rusaw

Problem Solving: Action Planning

675. New Owners: Planning Organizational Action, by Richard L. Bunning

Groups: How Groups Work

676. Logos: Taking Pride in Team Products, by Bonnie Jameson

Teams: How Groups Work

677. When Shall We Meet Again? Assessing Information in Teams, by Kristin J. Arnold

Teams: Problem Solving/Decision Making

678. Risk Tolerance: Understanding the Utility of Taking Risks, by Edward Earl Hampton, Jr.

Teams: Feedback

679. Nicknames: Summarizing What You Hear, by Michael P. Bochenek

Consulting and Facilitating: Facilitating: Opening

680. Age Barometer: Energizing a Group, by Robert Alan Black

Consulting and Facilitating: Facilitating: Skills

681. Trade Fair: Designing Job Aids, by W. Norman Gustafson

Leadership: Styles

682. Show and Tell: Learning About Leadership, by Richard T. Whelan

Locate other activities in these and other categories in the "Experiential Learning Activities Categories" chart that follows, or the comprehensive *Reference Guide to Handbooks and Annuals*. This book, which is updated regularly, indexes all of the *Annuals* and all of the *Handbooks of Structured Experiences* that we have published to date. With each revision, the *Reference Guide* becomes a complete, up-to-date, and easy-to-use resource for selecting appropriate materials from all of the *Annuals* and *Handbooks*.

EXPERIENTIAL LEARNING ACTIVITIES CATEGORIES

670. SPIRITUALITY AT WORK: AIDING PERSONAL GROWTH AND DEVELOPMENT

Goals

- To provide participants with an understanding of spiritual and personal growth at work.

- To provide an opportunity for participants to explore techniques for knowing themselves, connecting with others, and reaching their full potential.

Group Size

Ten to twenty people.

Time Required

Two to two and one half hours.

Materials

- One Spirituality at Work Key Learnings Sheet for each participant.

- One Spirituality at Work "What Are You Living For?" Worksheet for each participant.

- One Spirituality at Work Story Handout for each participant.

- One Spirituality at Work Self-Hypnosis Sheet for each participant.

- A flip chart and felt-tipped markers for the facilitator.

- Masking tape.

- Paper and pens or pencils for each participant.

Physical Setting

A room large enough for subgroups of four or five members each to work without distracting one another. If outdoor space is available, this might provide a desirable option for subgroups to explore.

Process

1. Begin by referencing the popularity of the Spirituality in the Workplace movement. Explain that, unfortunately, most employees are asked to leave their emotions and their souls at the front office door. This duality has created a separation of the "work self" from the "private self," which has created tension and stress both at work and in our private lives. State that we spend a great amount of our lives at work. However, most of us don't see work as a place for either personal development or spiritual fulfillment. Say that the workplace provides a great opportunity to gain insight about ourselves and to further our personal growth. (Five minutes.)

2. Distribute copies of the Spirituality at Work Key Learnings Sheet and read along with participants as you explain the following concepts more fully:

   "In order to self-awaken at work and re-establish a relationship with who we really are, there are three key learnings that must be understood and practiced:

   - *Know yourself:* The amount of depth within each of us has no boundary. Focus on learning and discovering you. Look deep inside and realize how wonderful you are.
   - *Connect with others:* We are all one. We are all the same. After we come to know ourselves, we can truly come to know and connect with others.
   - *Live to your potential:* How great you can be! Have you ever thought what living would be like if you were living to your potential?"

   Discuss what these concepts mean to people for a few minutes. (Five minutes.)

3. Explain that an important part of knowing yourself is understanding your life purpose and your purpose at work. Ask participants to raise their hands if they have developed a life purpose or a work purpose. Ask participants to share some examples. (Ten minutes.)

4. Distribute the Spirituality at Work "What Are You Living For?" Worksheet.

Ask participants to complete the worksheet individually. Explain that they may develop only some initial thoughts during this time rather than a scripted statement, which is completely acceptable. (Fifteen minutes.)

5. Form subgroups of three or four persons each. Ask the members of each subgroup to convene at a different table or to form their chairs into a small circle.

6. Ask the members of each subgroup to:

   - Take turns sharing their life/work purpose.

   - Take turns sharing how the process of developing the statement(s) worked for them.

   (Twenty minutes.)

7. Ask the subgroups to reassemble into one large group and debrief the activity by asking:

   - What insights or observations did you have from completing the worksheet?

   (Five minutes.)

8. Remind everyone that one critical piece of attaining personal fulfillment at work is *connecting with others*. One powerful way to connect with others is through sharing a personal story that is authentic. Explain that stories create an instant connection because you become vulnerable and accessible to others. Give a few examples of such stories. (Five minutes.)

9. Distribute the Spirituality at Work Story Handout and ask participants to read it. (Five minutes.)

10. Assemble participants into pairs and ask them to take turns sharing a personal story with their partners. (Ten minutes.)

11. Ask the pairs to reassemble into one large group and debrief by asking:

    - How did it feel to share a personal story with your partner?

    - What impact do you think sharing a personal story in the workplace might have on your working relationships?

    (Five minutes.)

12. Remind everyone that *realizing our own unique potential* is another way to achieve greater fulfillment and satisfaction at work. Say that a powerful technique for maximizing potential is self-hypnosis. Say that self-hypnosis is powerful because the subconscious mind cannot differentiate between

a real experience and a vividly imagined one. (Five minutes.)

13. Conduct a self-hypnosis demonstration with one or two volunteers by following the steps in the Spirituality at Work Self-Hypnosis Sheet to facilitate the exercise (do not give the sheet to participants at this point). (Fifteen minutes.)

14. Ask participants the following:

   ■ What do you think of the technique of self-hypnosis?

   ■ How did the experience go for you?

   ■ In what situations might self-hypnosis be valuable back on the job?

   (Five minutes.)

15. Distribute the Spirituality at Work Self-Hypnosis Sheet to participants and allow everyone to try the technique.

16. Ask participants whether they have any questions about conducting self-hypnosis and how the process went for them. Ask participants to share with partners. (Ten minutes.)

17. Bring the group together and review the importance of the three key learnings for personal growth and fulfillment at work (know yourself, connect with others, and realize your potential). To conclude, lead a discussion based on the following:

   ■ What are your key learnings from this session?

   ■ How might you use what you learned from these exercises in your work life?

   ■ How can you commit to using one of the techniques you have learned at work in the future?

   (Ten minutes.)

Variations

■ If the group size is small, that is, fewer than ten participants, have participants share their life/work purpose statements with the entire group rather than in small groups.

■ Reduce overall time and potential participant vulnerability by walking through the steps for self-hypnosis but eliminating the demonstration.

Submitted by Steven L. Phillips and Christina L. Collins.

Steven L. Phillips, Ph.D., *is well-known for his seminars, presentations, and consulting on organizational transformation, executive leadership, and the art of developing high-performance teams. He is a keynote speaker for conferences and organizations worldwide. Dr. Phillips is also well-known for behind-the-scenes executive coaching. He works one-on-one with presidents and CEOs, helping them strategize for powerful and successful leadership. His clients have included senior executives at Microsoft, PepsiCo, Disney, and Mattel.*

Christina L. Collins *is a principal consultant with Phillips Associates in Malibu, California. Ms. Collins is well-known for her seminars, presentations, and consulting on organizational change, communication, team development, and leadership. Her clients have included Viacom, Nestlé U.S.A., Pioneer Electronics, Mattel, and Jet Propulsion Laboratories.*

Spirituality at Work Key Learnings Sheet

To be the best we can, we must awaken our spirits. Notice that the word "awaken" is used instead of the words "develop" or "create." We must awaken the true self that already exists within us. It sounds easy, right? The challenge is that much of what we have learned has acted to disconnect us from our true selves. In order to self-awaken at work and to re-establish a relationship with who we really are, there are three key learnings that must be understood and practiced, as shown below.

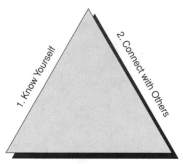

3. Live to Your Potential

Key Learnings for Awakening the Spirit

Know Yourself: The amount of depth within each of us has no boundary. Focus on learning and discovering you. Look deep inside and realize how wonderful you are.

Connect with Others: We are all one. We are all the same. After we come to know ourselves, we can truly come to know and connect with others.

Live to Your Potential: How great you can be! Have you ever thought what living would be like if you were living to your potential?

SPIRITUALITY AT WORK "WHAT ARE YOU LIVING FOR?" WORKSHEET

If you do not have an ultimate goal or sense of purpose, by default, you live to be comfortable. Having clarity is knowing what you are living for. Life is about moving toward your ultimate goal or moving away from it. People with a sense of purpose in life will have the greatest joy: A life with meaning.

Instructions: Fill in the answers to the questions below. Here are some examples that others have written:

Samples of Life Purpose	Samples of Work Purpose
Find truth	Develop my full potential
Love	Fight for a cause
Transcend nature	Help others see their strengths
Be a great person	Act in the service of others
Be happy	Lead
Find inner peace	Help humankind evolve

What are you living for (life purpose)?

What are you living for (work purpose)?

Spirituality at Work Story Handout

One powerful way to connect with others is to share something personal and real about yourself. Personal stories that are authentic create an instant connection with others because you become vulnerable and accessible in the telling. Don't try to paint yourself in a perfect light or tell your story just to impress someone else. Be real. Sharing a personal story creates trust between you and others because it shows you are willing to take a risk to further the connection.

Read the following examples of personal stories that create connection:

> "This morning my little boy crawled into bed with me right before I was ready to get up. Even though I had an early morning meeting and really could have used the extra fifteen minutes to get ready, when he looked at me with his big, brown eyes and said, 'Daddy, please stay a little longer,' my heart melted."

> "I remember being really nervous before giving my first formal presentation in a business environment. Even though I prepared and prepared, I still felt like I was going to be ill, especially when I realized that my boss had also decided to drop in on my presentation. Although I'm sure I made some mistakes, I got through it and it helped build my confidence that I could maybe even give another one."

Now read the following examples of personal stories that can create distance:

> "I know what it's like to feel late and rushed. Today my kid jumped in my bed and made me lose an extra fifteen minutes."

> "That was a nice job you did on that presentation. I remember my first presentation to the board; I wasn't even a bit nervous and I aced it. You should have seen the look on my boss's face when he realized that I did a better job then he did."

Practice sharing some personal stories of your own with others and notice the instant connection that is created.

SPIRITUALITY AT WORK SELF-HYPNOSIS SHEET

Self-hypnosis is a powerful tool for helping you reach your potential. The reason self-hypnosis is so powerful is because of the notion that the subconscious mind cannot differentiate between a real experience and a vividly imagined one. Try some self-hypnosis by following the steps below:

1. Pick something that you want to work on, for example, giving an effective presentation.

2. Get into a comfortable physical position. You may choose to lie on the floor.

3. Concentrate on relaxing your body. Close your eyes. Notice your breathing. Inhale through your nose and exhale through your mouth. Lengthen your breaths. Deepen your breaths. Now draw your breath into both the upper and lower back. Feel the rhythm and keep breathing.

4. Any outside sounds that you hear will help relax you further.

5. Let go of any thoughts that come into your mind.

6. Think of what you chose to work on for personal development and imagine it from two perspectives:

   ■ Watch yourself successfully doing what you want to work on from a 360-degree view above yourself. Visualize what success looks like from an outside perspective.

   ■ See yourself successfully doing what you want to work on through your own eyes. See and feel yourself being successful. See the event executed successfully from the start through completion. Watch yourself being successful over and over again.

   If you see yourself being unsuccessful, let go of judgment and then visualize the event being successful.

7. When you are ready, come out of the meditation slowly.

   ■ Feel where you are sitting.

   ■ Picture your surroundings.

   ■ Open your eyes, sit quietly, and adjust to your surroundings.

671. WHAT WORKS BEST?
IDENTIFYING LEARNING STYLES

Goals

- To identify participants' preferred styles for learning.
- To develop plans for professional growth using the identified learning styles.

Group Size

Up to thirty participants.

Time Required

Approximately two hours.

Materials

- A copy of What Works Best? Which Would You Choose? for each participant.
- A copy of What Works Best? Ways I've Learned in the Past for each participant.
- A copy of What Works Best? Categories of Learning Activities for each participant.
- A copy of What Works Best? Sample Professional Development Plan for each participant.
- A copy of What Works Best? Professional Development Plan for each participant.
- Blank paper and pencils for all participants.
- A flip chart and felt-tipped markers.

Physical Setting

Small tables with four or five chairs at each to accommodate the number of participants.

Process

1. Introduce the topic.

   "People who consciously plan their professional development usually gain results more quickly and systematically than do those who just let things happen."

   Tell a story about your own professional development or that of someone else that illustrates the point.

2. Explain that the goal of this activity is for participants to write their own professional development plans, and to do so in a way that they are most likely to be successful. Say:

   "The first step to planning any learning activity is to identify ways in which you learn best, so first, we'll review some specific ways you have learned well in situations in the past. Then you can incorporate this knowledge into a professional development plan of your own."

   (Four minutes.)

3. Give everyone copies of What Works Best? Which Would You Choose? Ask everyone to complete the worksheet quickly and quietly. (Five minutes.)

4. When everyone has finished, ask for a show of hands for each of the questions. Ask, "What did you observe about the answers from the group?" (They should note that responses varied quite a bit.) Write their observations on a flip chart. Summarize the various learning styles that have been identified.

5. Next, hand out copies of What Works Best? Ways I've Learned in the Past and ask everyone to complete the form as quickly and completely as possible. (Fifteen minutes.)

6. Ask participants to form groups of four or five at each table and share their answers to Questions 1 and 2 on the worksheet and to observe the variety of ways they have learned in the past. (Ten minutes.)

7. Solicit examples from each group and record them on the flip chart. (Five minutes.)

8. Ask for some examples of times when they were forced to learn in a style that did not fit their own style (Question 3 on the handout). (It is likely that many will indicate times when they were given lectures when they would have learned better with a hands-on activity.) (Five minutes.)

9. Poll people about their answers to Question 4. The question is based on Kolb's research on learning styles (Kolb, 1984). Give a short lecturette about learning style and draw examples from the participants as you review the four categories, writing each of the categories on the flip chart as you discuss it.

- Write "HOW?" on the flip chart.

   "If you answered A on Question 4, that you usually ask the question, *HOW does it work?* You learn best through *Concrete Experience* and choose to learn with actual examples, direct experience or field work, and activities that simulate real life."

- Write "WHY?" on the flip chart.

   "If you answered B to Question 4, you usually ask the question, *WHY do I want to learn this?* You learn best through *Reflection* and choose to learn with rhetorical or thought-promoting questions, discussions that probe deeply, or reflecting on 'why' through writing in a log or a journal."

- Write "WHAT?" on the flip chart.

   "If you answered C for Question 4, you usually ask the question, *WHAT am I learning here?* You learn best through *Abstract Conceptualization* and choose to learn through lectures, readings, or videos that outline the concept or model. Analogies work well for you too."

- Write "What If?" on the flip chart.

   "If you answered D for Question 4, you usually ask the question, *What if . . . ?* You learn best through *Active Experimentation* and choose to learn with hands-on activities. You would select on-the-job assignments, field or lab work, case studies, or simulations that give you the opportunity to put your skills or ideas into practice.

   "Kolb suggests that each of the four processes of learning should be present to ensure the most complete learning. Therefore, he encourages us to include some of each type of learning opportunity whenever we are trying to learn something new."

10. Distribute a copy of What Works Best? Categories of Learning Activities to each participant. Give a short lecturette about the major categories of learning, saying:

> "The Kolb model we just covered is only part of the picture about our learning preferences. When we recorded your examples on the flip chart of ways you've learned in the past, we noted the variety of activities we engage in as we learn.
>
> "Seven major categories of learning are listed on the handout. Follow along as we discuss them.
>
> 1. By attending classes, courses, training
>
> 2. Through self-directed learning
>
> 3. From other people
>
> 4. Through feedback
>
> 5. At professional events
>
> 6. From examples and models
>
> 7. By taking on assignments—learning by doing
>
> "Under each category are specific learning activities that we use. For example, under *Self-Directed Learning* you see the many ways people learn on their own: by using the Internet, using study guides, reading books, watching videos, or listening to audiotapes. Also, on our own we might reflect on mistakes we have made or evaluate our past actions and decisions.
>
> "You may discover that you select and use activities in a sequence. Let's say you want to learn how to use your new Palm Pilot. You first might read the manual, then second you might watch someone demonstrate how he or she uses one, and then third, you would give it a try."

   (Five to ten minutes.)

11. Ask participants to place a check mark beside those three or four categories of learning activity that they use most frequently, with no discussion.

12. In their same subgroups, ask them to share the learning methods they use most frequently. Poll the group and write on the flip chart which learning activities they use the most. Point out that the purpose of this lesson is to reaffirm how each person learns best and to use these learning activities whenever possible. (Ten minutes.)

13. Give everyone copies of the Sample Professional Development Plan to examine. Go over it with them to clarify the types of answers that have been filled in.

Explain that a *Goal* is a general area for professional development, such as "project management," "time management," "team development," and so on.

Objectives or *Outcomes* are more specific descriptions that identify a measurable behavior or skill learned. Objectives use action verbs such as those shown on the sample: "recognize, quantify, give, encourage."

Learning Activities are specific ways to achieve the stated objectives. Go over some possible objectives that the participants might have and write the objectives and some activities that could be used to accomplish the objective on the flip chart as examples in addition to those on the handout.

Measurements are concrete indicators of whether or not the objectives were achieved. Explain this concept with concrete examples in addition to those on the sample.

Timeline is the listing of when the learning activity will start and when it will end.

The box labeled "Done" is where the person would check off that an activity has been accomplished. (Ten minutes.)

14. When you have explained the sample thoroughly, give everyone blank paper to list two of their professional goals. They may do this by first listing up to ten professional goals and then narrowing the list down to the top two. (Ten minutes.)

15. Form groups of four and give each person a copy of the blank Professional Development Plan. Tell them to each take ten minutes to share their professional goals and preferred styles of learning. The other members of the subgroup are to make suggestions as the individual writes down appropriate learning activities that will accelerate the accomplishment of each of his or her professional goals. Tell the group members to help one another fill in measurement methods and check dates too. (Forty minutes.)

16. Ask for some sample goals and learning plans. The people in the total group might suggest some additional ideas too.

17. Summarize the lesson.

"We have explored the ways that each of us learns best. We have learned the value of selecting learning activities that match our preferences and style for learning so that our learning is enhanced."

Ask, "How can you use what we have just covered to help your own staff members accelerate their learning?" Listen to their ideas of how to transfer this process to others. Encourage them to select at least one person and in the very near future to lead that person through this process. By teaching someone else, they will reinforce what they have learned.

"Remember that because we are continuously learning, we can all strive to set our own professional goals and to decide how we accomplish them."

(Five minutes.)

Reference

Kolb, D.A. (1984). *Experiential learning: Experience as the source of learning and development.* Englewood Cliffs, NJ: Prentice Hall.

Submitted by Lois B. Hart.

Lois B. Hart, Ed.D., is president of Leadership Dynamics in Lafayette, Colorado, and director of the Women's Leadership Institute. Dr. Hart has over twenty-eight years' experience as a trainer, facilitator, and consultant presenting programs on leadership, teams, conflict, and facilitation. Dr. Hart earned her doctorate from the University of Massachusetts, where she studied organizational behavior and leadership with Dr. Kenneth Blanchard. She has authored twenty-one books, including 50 Activities for Developing Leaders, Learning from Conflict, Training Methods That Work, *and* Faultless Facilitation—A Resource Guide for Team and Group Leaders.

What Works Best? Which Would You Choose?

Instructions: For each of the questions below, order the answers from the method you would be most likely to use (1) to the method you would be least likely to use (4).

1. A new computer, VCR, or stereo you ordered has just arrived. After you remove all the parts from the shipping carton, what do you do next?

    _____ A. I set it up, plug it in, and start using it.

    _____ B. I think about how I've used a similar piece of equipment before and how that might relate to this new item.

    _____ C. I read the manual.

    _____ D. I ask someone who has experience to help me set it up.

2. Your organization is launching a new initiative to introduce teams into everyday work. How would you learn best about teams?

    _____ A. By reading.

    _____ B. By listening to audiotapes or lectures.

    _____ C. By discussing the ideas and techniques with others.

    _____ D. By trying the ideas out.

What Works Best? Ways I've Learned in the Past

Instructions: For the each item below, think of similar situations you have been in and answer the questions about what worked best for you.

1. Name a time you learned a great deal, whether it was a short-term experience or a long-term experience. What were you learning?

   Who determined what you were to learn?

   How did you learn the material or process? What was the outcome?

2. Name a skill, idea, or concept that you have learned this past year (job related, a personal interest, or a hobby).

   How did you learn?

   What was the outcome?

3. What happens when you are forced by others or circumstances to learn using a style that is different from your preferred style?

4. When you need to learn something new, which of these questions do you ask yourself?

A. "HOW does it work?"

B. "WHY am I learning this?"

C. "WHAT will I do with this knowledge?"

D. "What if. . .?"

WHAT WORKS BEST? CATEGORIES OF LEARNING ACTIVITIES

Instructions: Let's examine some categories of learning activities that you could use for your professional development. Put a check mark below in front of each method you like to use.

Classes, Courses, Training

———— ■ Classes at universities and colleges

———— ■ Training programs

Self-Directed Learning

———— ■ Internet

———— ■ Computer programs

———— ■ Study guides

———— ■ Books

———— ■ Audiotapes

———— ■ Videos

———— ■ Learn from mistakes, inappropriate decisions, or behavior from people such as my boss, colleagues, employees, professional mentor, coach, personal friend or intimates, or public figures

Other People

———— ■ Mentor

———— ■ Seek individuals for ideas

———— ■ Seek a coach for more assistance

———— ■ Start a professional group

———— ■ Interview

———— ■ Observe

Feedback

———— ■ Self-administered instruments/assessments

———— ■ 360-degree feedback instruments/assessments

_____ ■ Surveys—organizational, team, customer

_____ ■ Solicit feedback from others

_____ ■ Teach and then solicit the learners' feedback

Professional Events

_____ ■ Conferences

_____ ■ Association meetings and events

From Example and Models

_____ ■ Field visits

_____ ■ Benchmark programs and other companies

_____ ■ Review data or history

Assignments—Learn by Doing

_____ ■ Special assignments

_____ ■ Job rotation: change job function, division, lines of business

_____ ■ Work on or lead task forces, action teams

_____ ■ Lead a project

_____ ■ Lead a turnaround or fix a process

_____ ■ Volunteer in a community group

WHAT WORKS BEST? SAMPLE PROFESSIONAL DEVELOPMENT PLAN

Goal: Increased Rewards and Recognition of My Employees

Objectives or Outcomes	Learning Activities	Measurements	Timeline	Done
To recognize my direct reports more often	Review ways I could recognize them more by reading Nelson's book: *1001 Ways to Reward Employees*	After reading the book, select the five best ideas	12/1–12/15	
To quantify how often I currently recognize others	For one week, I will keep track in my day planner whenever I recognize someone and how I did it.	Completed log	12/8–12/13	
To give public recognition to others	Make place on staff meeting agenda to praise individuals or teams publicly	Line item for this on each agenda	start on 12/16	
To give a minimum of one verbal positive comment to each of my direct reports each week	Make a list of positive phrases I would be comfortable saying	Keep a tally for one month (It takes a month to start a new habit)	12/21–1/21	
To encourage my staff to also recognize others	I will lead by example. I will praise individuals who give others some form of recognition. I'll coach those who don't.	Do assessment of each person	Now and in three months	

WHAT WORKS BEST? PROFESSIONAL DEVELOPMENT PLAN

Instructions: Complete the development plan below for yourself.

Name: _____

Date: _____

Goal (Area I Wish to Develop): _____

Objectives or Outcomes	Learning Activities	Measurements	Timeline	Done

672. Passion and Purpose: Helping Employees Realign with the Organization

Goals

- To offer the participants an opportunity to examine their passion for work.

- To offer the participants an opportunity to examine what they perceive to be their purpose in life.

- To help align individuals' passion and purpose with organizational goals.

Group Size

A group of six to twenty participants. Individuals need not be from the same organization.

Time Required

Approximately three hours.

Materials

- A copy of the Passion and Purpose Passion Inventory for each participant.

- A copy of the Passion and Purpose Purpose Worksheet for each participant.

- A copy of the Passion and Purpose Alignment Worksheet for each participant.

- A pen or pencil for each participant.

- A flip chart and felt-tipped markers.

Physical Setting

A large room with tables and chairs with plenty of space for subgroups to discuss without disturbing one another.

Process

1. Announce the goals of the activity.

2. Open with the following brief comment about the importance of reflecting on passion and purpose in one's life:

   "To discover your purpose, you must discover how to live from the inside out, that is, no one can tell you your purpose, it has to come from within yourself. You need to discover your strengths and weaknesses, discover what motivates you, discover where your passions lie. A discovery process like this does not happen easily. You must spend some time, do some soul searching, and want to do it.

   "*Purpose* is the deepest dimension within us. It resides deep inside each one of us. It gives us a sense of direction—a way of life—and helps us to discover why we are here. *Passion* is the motivation we feel when we discover our purpose. Once we know what our purpose is, passion takes over to help us accomplish it."

3. Hand out the Passion and Purpose Passion Inventory and pens or pencils. Have all participants complete it independently. (Five minutes.)

4. Ask participants to find a partner with whom they will share insights they gained from completing the Inventory. (Fifteen minutes.)

5. After all participants have had a chance to share with a partner, ask the whole group for common themes and elements. Write these on a flip chart under the heading "Passion." (Fifteen minutes.)

6. Hand out the Passion and Purpose Purpose Worksheet. Again, ask each participant to complete it individually. (Ten minutes.)

7. Ask participants to find a partner with whom they will share insights they gained from completing the Purpose Worksheet. (Fifteen minutes.)

8. Ask each pair to join with another so there are now four people in a group. Again, ask them to come up with insights regarding their purpose. (Twenty minutes.)

9. After all participants have had a chance to share within the larger subgroup, ask the whole group for common themes and elements. Write these on a flip chart under the heading "Purpose." (Fifteen minutes.)

10. Next, ask the whole group to look at the two flip-chart pages. Ask them to make connections between what they listed about passion and what is listed regarding purpose. Write their observations on another piece of flip-chart paper under the heading "Passion and Purpose." (Fifteen minutes.)

11. Give a Passion and Purpose Alignment Worksheet to each participant. Have each person work with a partner to complete the worksheet. Ask the partners to help one another develop plans for aligning passion with purpose. (Fifteen minutes.)

12. After pairs have had time to work on individual plans, ask the whole group for additional insights, using such questions as:

   ■ Is your plan feasible?

   ■ What barriers exist to attaining your goals?

   ■ Where did you have to compromise?

   ■ Do you need to make major changes? If so, what kind?

   (Fifteen minutes.)

13. Summarize major points from the entire group. (Ten minutes.)

Variations

■ To save time, participants can be asked to complete the Passion Inventory and Purpose Worksheet before they come to the session.

■ This workshop can be done within one organization, across organizations, or for personal development outside of the workplace.

Submitted by Patricia Boverie and Michael Kroth.

Patricia Boverie is an associate professor of organizational learning and instructional technologies at the University of New Mexico. She teaches courses in adult learning theory, consulting, organization development, and team/group learning and development. She holds a Ph.D. from the University of Texas at Austin. Dr. Boverie's areas of expertise are in the fields of individual, team, and organizational learning. Her current research interest is in examining passion and its relationship to work. She also has a private consulting practice.

Michael Kroth *is a senior organizational consultant at Public Service Company of New Mexico, and he has his own training, development, and public presentation business. He received his BFA in theater arts and an MBA and Ph.D. in training and learning technologies from the University of New Mexico. Dr. Kroth has facilitated training and interventions at the local, state, and national level. He teaches part-time for the University of New Mexico and is conducting research on the changing workforce and passion.*

PASSION AND PURPOSE PASSION INVENTORY

Instructions: Answer each of the following based on how true it is for you by making a check mark in the appropriate column.

Not True	Some-what True	Very True	
——	——	——	1. I have a sense of passion for my work.
——	——	——	2. I have a strong motivation to work.
——	——	——	3. I am living my dreams.
——	——	——	4. I feel that my life truly matters.
——	——	——	5. Every Monday I go to work energized and eager to begin another work week.
——	——	——	6. I have a personal calling to do the work I do.
——	——	——	7. I am fortunate that I can use my special talents in my work.
——	——	——	8. I value the people with whom I work.
——	——	——	9. I am able to make a living doing what I most love to do.
——	——	——	10. I nearly always go to bed at night feeling that I had a good day at work.

PASSION AND PURPOSE PURPOSE WORKSHEET

Instructions: Complete the worksheet by giving short answers, but examining the topic in as much depth as possible. You will be discussing your answers with a partner and then in small groups, so these are simply conversation starters, not essay answers.

What do you most love to do?

What are some things you would love to be able to do with your life?

What are the most important things in your life at this time?

What special talents, personality characteristics, or abilities do you possess?

List three of your favorite things to do in your spare time:
1.
2.
3.

What about each of these things brings you joy?

Do they have anything in common?

If you could go back and change one direction your life has taken, what would you change?

When your life is over, what would you like people to say about you?

What do you think is your purpose in life?

Do you feel that purpose as a burning desire inside of you?

Does your purpose keep you interested and energized, even when others give up or burn out?

Would you pursue your passion, even if you were not paid to do so?

By achieving your purpose, would you instill passion in other people?

Would other people come to you to find out what your "secret" is?

PASSION AND PURPOSE ALIGNMENT WORKSHEET

Instructions: Complete the worksheet in preparation for a discussion with a partner, who will help you find ways to align your passion and your purpose.

Organizational Mission (if known):

Departmental Mission/Goals:

Personal Purpose/Goals:

What personal goals do you have in common with your organization or department?

Where are your own goals not in congruence with those of your workplace?

What steps could you take to realign your personal goals with those of the workplace?

Are the goals so incongruent that you should seek another line of work? If so, where are you likely to find a line of work that is in balance with your own passion?

673. WORKPLACE SCENARIOS: DEALING WITH EMOTIONAL BEHAVIOR

Goals

- To identify causes of emotional behavior in the workplace.
- To raise awareness of language that can cause emotional escalation of a situation.
- To provide strategies for defusing emotional situations.

Group Size

Eighteen to twenty-four.

Time Required

Two to three hours, depending on options selected.

Materials

- One copy of the Workplace Scenarios Lecturette for the facilitator
- Two or three copies of the Workplace Scenarios Observation Sheet for each participant, depending on whether there are three or four participants per group.
- One Workplace Scenarios Situations Sheet for each participant.
- Blank paper for each participant.
- Pencils or pens for participants.
- Name tents for each participant.
- One flip-chart easel with newsprint pad.
- Various colored felt-tipped markers.
- Masking tape.

Physical Setting

A room large enough for group discussion, for small groups to gather for brainstorming sessions, and for groups of three to four participants to practice their skill activities.

Process

1. Lead a facilitated discussion based on the Workplace Scenarios Lecturette. You may hand out copies of this lecturette for participants to keep if you desire.

2. At various points in the discussion, stop and either form small groups or lead a large group brainstorming activity on topics you select from the material. For each activity, allow approximately five to ten minutes for the groups to brainstorm and for you to post their ideas. The following are possible topics for brainstorming:

   ■ Additional external factors that contribute to emotional behavior in the workplace.

   ■ Additional internal factors that contribute to emotional behavior in the workplace.

   ■ Additional "hot buttons" that can lead to emotional behavior.

   ■ Additional empathy statements that could be used.

   ■ Additional feel/felt statements that one could use.

3. At the end of the facilitated discussion, summarize the points you have made on a flip chart so that participants can refer to them easily. Separate participants into groups of three or four. Explain that each participant will have an opportunity to practice the skills learned using at least two or three of the strategies you have discussed for handling emotional behavior. Tell participants that one person will practice while the others serve as observers or as role players with the person practicing the behavior. If there are four people in a group, there will be two observers.

4. Provide each participant with enough Workplace Scenario Observation Sheets so that they have one for each of the other participants in their group (either two or three). Tell them to read the instructions on their sheets and to observe their teammates to capture specific things that are done during the practice sessions.

5. Give everyone a copy of the Workplace Scenarios Situations Sheet and tell them to review the three situations, selecting the one that they would like to practice.

6. Have participants volunteer for roles within their subgroups (one practicing participant, one practice partner, and one or two observers).

7. When everyone is ready, tell participants they have ten minutes per person to practice a scenario and then have their peers give them feedback on their use of skills. Also, tell them that, after the first practicing participant has completed his or her scenario and received peer feedback, that each member of the group should turn his or her name tent on end lengthwise. This will signal that the group is finished. They should not proceed until told to do so. (Ten minutes.)

8. Once all name tents are on end, debrief this portion of the activity by asking everyone:

   ■ What worked well?

   ■ What would you do differently if you were to repeat the same scenario?

   ■ What did you learn from this activity?

9. Now instruct participants to change roles in their groups and proceed. Once the second participant has finished practicing, groups should continue with the next and so on until all participants have practiced their skills and received peer feedback. (Twenty or thirty minutes.)

10. As participants practice, keep time, informing the group when there are two minutes left. Additionally, make mental notes on what you hear. Comment on these things at the end of the group practice session.

11. After all participants have had a chance to practice their skills debrief the entire group by asking:

   ■ What worked well?

   ■ What was difficult?

   ■ What general comments do you have about the activity?

   ■ What did you learn from the activity and discussion?

   ■ How will you use what was learned in the workplace or in dealing with emotional people in the future?

Variations

- Supplement the facilitated discussion by including additional information on any of the topic areas (e.g., listening, questioning, verbal and nonverbal cues, defusing techniques, or feedback). Select additional materials by determining the needs of participants or the organization.

- In preparation for the session, have participants log onto the Internet or otherwise research any of the topics addressed in the lecturette. Ask participants either to present their findings in small groups or to the group as a whole. They could also distribute printed copies of the information before or during the session.

- Instead of using the practice scenarios provided, participants could identify specific actual workplace issues that they want to address. Before each practice begins, the practicing participant would then brief other group members about the actual situation, anticipated behavior, and how they expect other parties to react. This allows practicing partners to know how to interact during the practice session and for observers to know what to look for.

References

Blanchard, K., & Johnson, S. (1982). *The one minute manager.* New York: Berkley Books.

Fullerton, H.N., Jr. (1997, November). Labor force 2006: Slowing down and changing composition. *Monthly Labor Review:* Washington, DC: Bureau of Labor Statistics, U.S. Department of Labor, p 1.

Mehrabion, A. (1968, September). Communicating Without Words. *Psychology Today,* pp. 52–55.

Submitted by Robert William Lucas.

Robert William Lucas is president of Creative Presentation Resources, Inc., in Casselberry, Florida. He has nearly three decades' experience working with all types of organizations as a manager and trainer. Mr. Lucas was the 1995 president of the Central Florida Chapter of ASTD, the 1999/2000 chairperson of Leadership Seminole, appears in Who's Who in the World, Who's Who in the United States, *and* Who's Who in the South and Southeast. *He is the author of seven books, including* Customer Service Skills *and* Concepts for Business. *His latest book,* Customer Service for the 21st Century: Skills and Concepts for Success, *is scheduled for release in 2000.*

WORKPLACE SCENARIOS LECTURETTE

Emotional reactions are normal human responses to situations, whether in or out of the workplace. Dealing with them takes time, patience, skill, and practice on the part of managers, co-workers, and others. Unfortunately, many people have few if any of the basic skills required, no patience, no time, and little practice. Additionally, many people have an aversion to dealing with others who become emotional easily. The reality is that by avoiding emotional situations and people who may become emotional, they potentially increase the likelihood that another person's emotions will either escalate or smolder and erupt again later. Depending on the severity of the situation, there is potential for even more severe and violent outbursts from the person at a later time.

Causes of Emotional Behavior

In an ever-changing, diverse, highly technical work environment, many factors can contribute to stress and/or heightened emotions. Although some of these are environmental factors and thus out of any one person's control, others are not. Basically, the factors that usually can be controlled or confronted fall into two categories: *external* (often out of the emotional person's control) and *internal* (often within that person's control).

External Factors

Environment. Sometimes the environment in which people choose to have meetings or provide feedback is not conducive to open communication. This, coupled with poorly timed messages, discussed later, are surefire ways to lead to confrontation. For example, if a co-worker made an error with a customer order, standing in line in the cafeteria while his or her friends are around may not be the time to convey that fact to them. A more appropriate location would be a private room or isolated area in the workplace.

Time. Everyone has the same amount of time each day (86,400 seconds, 1,440 minutes, or 24 hours). Some people use their time more efficiently than others do. Depending on the type of work environment in which people find themselves, there may be increased stress because of time usage. For example, people working in production areas (manufacturing, sales, or call centers) in which they are held accountable for production rates have timed standards for productivity or work at a hectic pace. They can be severely impacted by such external factors. Another example might occur in an environment in which there are high levels of stress due to an inadequate number of employees handling the workload. This can create a situation in which employees have to work extended amounts of overtime or on weekends. The result is often that people have little time to think before they speak or to think before reacting.

Timing.   Picking the right time to hold a conversation or provide feedback to someone is very important. Choosing the wrong moment, when the person is hurried or already emotionally charged, can lead to an emotional outburst. For example, if a co-worker, boss, or client has just had a negative encounter with someone else, is on a tight deadline, or had some personal tragedy occur, he or she is most likely not ready for feedback on performance. If someone has just gotten off the telephone with an angry person, he or she may not be in a frame of mind to listen to feedback about how he or she dealt with that caller.

Technology.   Although technology can increase effectiveness and efficiency under the proper circumstances, it can also add more stress to people's lives. For example, if workers are already understaffed with tight deadlines and their employer introduces new hardware or software, problems can erupt. This is especially true when inadequate training and technical support are provided to help employees deal with the new systems.

Other People.   Whenever two or more people come into contact, there is an opportunity for a breakdown in communication and conflict. This is because each person brings a whole list of issues that can cause differences of opinion (for example, diversity of age, race, gender, cultural background, sexual preference, skill at interpersonal communication, values, beliefs, and many other factors).

Internal Factors

Circadian Rhythm.   Each human has an internal twenty-four hour "biological clock" that is affected by the rotational pull of the earth as night changes to day and back again. Much research has been done on the impact of this cycle and how it affects people differently. People are typically categorized as "morning people" if their systems work more efficiently in the early hours of the day. They tend to wake earlier, more refreshed, and are ready to face the challenges of the day immediately. As the day goes on, they often tend to feel more sluggish and become less alert. Afternoons are definitely not their peak time for meetings, discussion, or receiving feedback. On the other hand, "evening people" are just hitting their stride mid-day or later and often stay up and/or work later.

Recognizing the cycle of their own body and that of those around them can help people deal more efficiently with co-workers, family members, and those with whom they interact regularly. It can also assist them in choosing the proper time of day to engage certain people in a variety of ways. For example, if a manager recognizes that the majority of employees are morning people, yet consistently schedules staff meetings for 4 p.m. on Friday, the manager is asking for a loss of efficiency and meeting with people who are tired and emotionally not receptive to feedback. A more positive approach might be to have lunch meetings when the morning people are still alert and the evening people are just coming into their prime period for receptiveness.

Cultural Background.   Each day, the number of people entering the workplace from different cultures increases. For example, the U.S. Department of Labor estimates that by the year 2006 the number of Hispanic workers will equal the number of African-Americans, while the Asian worker population will expand more rapidly than any other. At the same time, women will grow from 46 to 47 percent of the worker population (Fullerton, 1997). The impact of these shifts is that there is a crucial need for employees to understand not only the differences, but also the similarities in people. They also need to learn more about the values and beliefs of others so that there is a better understanding of why people act a certain way and do things as they do. Only through understanding and better communication can conflict and breakdowns in relationships be reduced.

Behavioral Style Preference.   Numerous self-assessment instruments (surveys) are available to help people determine their own behavioral style preferences or temperaments. Such factors have been measured for hundreds of years in an effort to categorize human behavior. Although there is not an absolute measure due to the uniqueness of humans, many of these surveys are valuable in raising self-awareness and pointing out common characteristics. Once a person becomes aware of the type of behaviors he or she exhibits in various situations, it becomes easier to adapt, if needed. It is also easier to spot similar or different behaviors in others and to modify the approach used in dealing with those people.

Interpersonal Communication Skills.   Communication skills are learned. Unfortunately, some people have not learned as well as others. For effective relationship building to occur in any situation, people must master such skills as listening, verbal and nonverbal communication, networking, and conflict management. Each of these types of skills is crucial in being able to receive and give feedback, ask questions, gather information, and resolve disagreements effectively. Each skill set involves an active process that must be learned and mastered through effective practice. The more a person learns and practices, the more likely he or she is to improve.

Values and Beliefs. Like interpersonal communication skills, values and beliefs are taught. Parents, family members, clergy, educators, books, television, printed materials, and many other sources contribute to what each person thinks is good or bad, right or wrong, and valuable or invaluable. When people come into contact with others who have different values and beliefs, arguments and differences of opinion are possible. And, if left unchecked, such differences can escalate into an emotional confrontation.

Dealing with Emotional Behavior

Effective interpersonal communication skills are the key to addressing emotional situations. Through such skills as active listening, questioning in a non-threatening manner, and providing feedback that is directed at behavior or issues rather than at the person, many emotional encounters can be avoided, reduced, or eliminated.

Active Listening

As discussed earlier, listening well is a learned skill. It is also the primary means that most people use to gather information. Many people fail to recognize this fact and assume that they automatically know how to listen because they "hear" what someone said. In reality, *hearing* is a passive process (done unconsciously) that requires little or no effort when a person has a normal range of hearing and no hearing impairments.

On the other hand, *listening* is an active process (consciously done) that begins with *hearing*. Once sounds are heard or received, the brain goes to work *attending* to what was heard and trying to filter out other sounds so that it can focus on the exact incoming message. The next step in the listening process is *comprehending* or *assigning meaning* to the message by matching it to information already stored in the brain. After a match is found and the brain makes sense of the message, *responding* takes place (either verbally or nonverbally). This response may also be to do or say nothing, based on the original incoming message.

If this process is not completed effectively because other factors interrupted any stage of it or emotions got in the way, effective and productive two-way communication does not occur. When the cause is emotional, inappropriate reactions typically occur because incomplete information has been gathered for a response.

Verbal Communication Skills

Like listening, verbal communication involves skills that must be learned and practiced effectively. A number of subskills are involved. Each requires a thorough understanding of the concept and a conscious effort to use it. The following are some of the skills involved in verbal two-way communication, along with some examples of how to use them in emotional situations.

Questioning

Many variations of questions can be used; however, they generally fall into two categories *open-ended* and *closed*.

Open-ended questions typically start with words like what, when, how, and why. They are designed to engage the listener, create open dialogue, solicit ideas or input, or gather large amounts of information.

Examples

- What do you think about this idea?
- When do you think is the best time to start the project?
- How are you today?
- Why do you believe that?

Closed-end questions typically begin with a verb (e.g., will, can, do, are, may, or should) and often result in short responses, such as one-syllable answers, a number, yes or no, or acknowledgements (e.g., uh-huh, okay, or right).

Examples

- Will this be the last time you will order this product?
- May I see the project plan?
- Do you have time to talk right now?
- Are you asking for one or two?
- May I call to schedule an appointment for tomorrow?
- Should I give this to your assistant?

A point to remember when asking questions is that you typically get what you ask for (and sometimes more). Additionally, if you ask the wrong type of question at the wrong time, or ask the wrong person, you may evoke an emotional response. For example, assume that you are a salesperson who is calling on a regular customer who had a problem with his last two orders. Why do you think the customer is reacting in the following manner?

> *You:* "Good morning, Mr. Smolinski. (Smiling) How are you today?" (Open-ended)
>
> *Mr. Smolinski:* "Okay. (Not smiling) Did you get that problem straightened out yet?" (Closed-end)
>
> *You:* "Well, I've . . . ummm . . . been checking on it. Didn't you call my office to check with my assistant?" (A closed-end question starting with a negative)
>
> *Mr. Smolinski:* "Call your office! Why should I call anywhere?" (Open-ended)
>
> *You:* "I only meant that I thought after our last meeting you would follow up to check the status. I can check it for you right now. Is that all right?" (Closed-end)
>
> *Mr. Smolinski:* "Why in the world do you think I'd check on the status?! It's YOUR problem! Of course it's all right."

Several things are happening here. The first is that the customer is frustrated because he's had an ongoing issue that you have not resolved. Second, your approach is rather upbeat and your responses unassertive. Also, you asked a negative, leading, closed-end question to determine what action the customer had taken. He views this as your problem, and you apparently do not seem to be taking ownership. In such instances, the approach taken is very likely to lead to escalation of a situation.

Let's see how this might have gone differently:

> *You:* "Good morning, Mr. Smolinski. (Smiling) I hope you are well today. (No question requesting input until you are ready) I want you to know that I have not forgotten about the problem we have had with your orders. I have been checking on the situation." (Assumes that this ongoing issue will be a prime topic of discussion, subconsciously partners with the customer on the issue through the use of the pronoun "we," and takes a proactive approach, as opposed to the reactive, avoidance method used in the last example)

> *Mr. Smolinski:* "Good. (Not smiling) When can I expect the problem to be resolved?" (Closed-end)
>
> > *You:* "I don't have that answer yet, but should know by . . . . Does that sound all right to you?" (Closed-end question to control the conversation and gain commitment)
>
> *Mr. Smolinski:* "I guess that will be fine, but I cannot wait any longer than that."
>
> > *You:* "I understand how important this is. Rest assured, I'll keep working on it personally. Is there anything else I can do for you today?" (Empathy statement to show compassion, assurance of personal action, and controlling the conversation with a closed-end question)
>
> *Mr. Smolinski:* "Good. No, there isn't. Thanks."

Notice that by using the defusing techniques of empathizing and assuring, coupled with controlling closed-end questions, you are able to better guide the conversation. There is less input, so there is reduced opportunity for emotional escalation. However, in other situations when a person is highly emotional, the person should be encouraged to vent through your use of active listening and open-ended questioning.

Rapport-Building Techniques

Empathy is a good strategy to show someone who is emotional that you can see the issue from his or her perspective. In effect, you are verbally "walking a mile in another's shoes," showing that you can relate to what he or she is saying or to the situation.

Effective customer service providers often use this technique. It is a great strategy to help bond with an emotional person; however, you must sound sincere or you might inadvertently send the person off to a higher emotional level. If you cannot truly see the point, don't say you can. Also, if you have never been in a situation similar to the person's, be careful about saying you can understand how he or she feels. The person may call you on it by asking, "How can you possibly know how I feel? Has [whatever the situation] ever happened to you?" If you say, "No," then the person's emotions could escalate, his or her anger could be focused on you, and your credibility would be destroyed.

Here are some typical phrases that show empathy:

- I understand that you are concerned.

- I know how you feel.

- I can appreciate how you feel (Much better than "understand" or "know," as it simply recognizes the emotion without putting you in a similar situation).

- I recognize how frustrating this must be.

- I cannot blame you for thinking that.

- I see what you mean.

Feel/felt-found is a technique that has been used by salespeople for years to connect subconsciously with customers. It is a technique that often ties directly to the empathy strategy just described. By using it, you can help people mentally connect to a larger group because they now recognize that others have felt the same way under similar circumstances. For example, if a salesperson were trying to persuade a customer to purchase a new six-disk CD player for his or her car, but the customer offered an objection of, "I really don't know if I need a player with that many disks," using the feel/felt method, coupled with the empathy approach from earlier, the salesperson might respond: "I can understand how you might believe that, Mr. Thomas. Many other people have felt that way when deciding on a model [the salesperson has empathized with the customer]. However, many people have found that the added convenience and enhanced safety of not having to wrestle with CD cases while they are driving down the road is well worth the extra dollars that this unit costs." (Appealing to the customer's analytical common sense while connecting the person with other prudent customers).

When dealing with an emotional person, the combined techniques of empathy and feel/felt-found might look like this:

> *Customer:* "I've had it with your delays. You promised me a week ago that I'd have the products I ordered, but I still don't have them. Doesn't anyone in your company honor promises made to customers?"

> *You:* "Ms. Rodriguez, I can appreciate your frustration. I'd feel that way too if I were you; however, if you just give me one more day, I'm sure you'll find that our company does follow through on its promises." (Empathy, feel/felt-found)

> *Customer:* "Okay, you have one more day; then I'm canceling my
> order."
>
> *You:* "Thank you, I'll deliver it myself." (Showing appreciation)

Note: In this example, you did not let the customer pull you into a verbal confrontation, even when she suggested that you lied to her. By staying in control of your emotions and using the rapport-building techniques followed by a show of appreciation, you controlled an emotional situation.

Defusing Techniques

Rational responses are a way to help keep the emotional level down for all parties involved in an emotional situation. An important part of this technique is for a person to recognize his or her own "hot buttons," words and actions that tend to cause escalated emotions. Some examples might be the following words and phrases:

You must/should	You're wrong/mistaken
I/you can't	What's your problem?
No	You always/never
You'll have to	Policy says/prohibits

I'm sorry or I apologize (without reason for feeling sorry or apology)

Once people recognize that these words and phrases can trap them emotionally, they are on the way to avoiding conflict by using rational responses. There are varieties of these responses: directional questions, logic statements, information statements, and option statements.

Directional questions attempt to guide someone from an emotional level to a more rational one. (See the questioning section below.)

Logic statements consist of appeals to the person's intellect through statements of fact. These can be coupled with questions to gauge how receptive the person is. For example, in dealing with an emotional person who already filled out a loan application that was subsequently lost by an employee of a bank, the following exchange might occur between a bank supervisor and the customer: "I understand your frustration. I'd be frustrated too if this happened to me; however, unless we have the information to forward to our loan officer, your request cannot be processed. I promise that this one will not get lost; I'll handle it myself. So, can I please impose on you to complete the form one more time." (Combination of Feel/Felt with appeal to logic followed by closed-end question.)

Informational statements add "meat" to other comments. For example, if someone is upset because of an organizational error, she might expect some sort of apology and ultimately atonement for the trouble created. If a service provider simply says, "I'm sorry" or "I apologize" without an informational statement connected, the customer could become more upset. He or she might even respond sarcastically, "I know you're sorry. So is everyone else in this stupid company! Now what are you going to do to fix the problem you created?!"

A simple way that such an outburst might be avoided would be to say something like the following: "I'm sorry for the inconvenience we've caused by not delivering the right sofa. I appreciate why you're upset; I'd be upset too. I can assure you that we are going to have the one you ordered at your house by 3 p.m. today, and we'll pick up the other one. Please accept my apologies." (Apology with informational statement, empathy statement, reassurance, and second apology.)

Option statements provide alternatives for someone who is unhappy or emotional about a situation. It is a subtle way of compensating them for being inconvenienced. It also lets them feel in control of the situation by allowing them to make a choice, for example: "I'm sorry that the color you wanted is out of stock. We've sold a lot of this item since the sale started. I'd be happy to take your name and phone number and call you when replacements come in, or if you would like to purchase and pay for it now, I'll have it delivered once replacements arrive. Which would you prefer?" (Apology, followed by information statement, and variation statement.)

Nonverbal Communication Skills

Nonverbal cues (posture, arm, hand, and head gestures, facial expressions, environmental cues) are often similar from person to person; however, they can send different messages. This is because when people receive nonverbal cues they may have different interpretations of the meaning of the signal. For example, someone might use a curled fisted with a thumb pointed up in the air to indicate "everything is okay"; however, the receiver of the gesture is from Nigeria and becomes upset. Why? In that country, the gesture is rude. This is one reason why an understanding of diversity is so important in establishing and maintaining relationships.

Just as with any aspect of interpersonal communication, there will often be room for misinterpretation. This is why nonverbal cues (e.g., gestures, facial expressions, and appearance) are so powerful. In one classic study, Dr. Albert Mehrabian (1968) found that in an interaction between two people, more emotion is transmitted through nonverbal means than from the words spoken. The results were that 55 percent of message meaning comes from nonverbal cues, 38 percent from vocal cues (e.g., rate of speech, volume, tone, pitch, etc.), and only 7 percent from the words chosen. This should not be interpreted to mean that words are not important. On the contrary, they are very powerful, depending on how they are used. The numbers simply mean that when a verbal and nonverbal message are used simultaneously, more credence is given to the nonverbal than to the verbal. That is why verbal messages should match, that is, be in congruence with, nonverbal components of a communication.

Because nonverbal cues communicate so much message meaning, it is often easy to detect a person's emotional state by the signals he or she sends. For example, if people are happy, they will likely have an upbeat tone to their voices and smile a lot. On the other hand, if they are angry or emotionally distraught, they may exhibit some or all of the following mannerisms in an attempt to show displeasure, intimidate, or demean another person:

- Invading personal space (often within a distance of two feet or less);
- Pointing (with fingers or objects);
- Leaning or hovering above someone who is seated (using height to intimidate or control);
- Throwing objects;
- Pounding a fist on a surface;
- Using a loud voice;
- Sighing loudly;
- Using offensive gestures; or
- Physically touching or pushing someone.

Recognizing such signals as indicators of high emotion can help in the avoidance or defusion of confrontations or unpleasant situations.

Feedback

In his book, *The One Minute Manager,* Ken Blanchard (1982) says that "Feedback is the breakfast of champions." Without effective feedback, two-way communication cannot occur. Feedback provides the information on how a message was received. Feedback may be in either verbal or nonverbal form. In situations of high emotion, it is crucial both to listen actively and to observe nonverbal cues closely in an effort to gauge a speaker's state. Based on the interpretation of messages received, a person can then plan an appropriate, nonthreatening response or attempt to defuse the situation, if necessary.

Here is an example of how feedback might work in an emotional encounter with an upset co-worker who has just stormed into your office and slammed a notepad on your desk.

> *You:* "Manuel, you seem very upset. What's wrong?" (Recognize the emotion and offer to assist)
>
> *Manuel:* "I've had it with this place! People don't care about customers and they certainly don't care about their co-workers."
>
> *You:* "I'm not sure I understand. What do you mean?" (Open-ended question)
>
> *Manuel:* "Last week, Jennifer said she would handle a customer problem I had. She said she would research the issue and follow up with the customer."
>
> *You:* "Yes. So what happened?" (Open-ended)
>
> *Manuel:* "I just got a call from the customer. He read me the riot act, called me every name in the book, said he'd never do business with us again, and that he is going to write the CEO a letter!"
>
> *You:* "Wow! I can see why you are upset. I'd be upset too. What did Jennifer say about all this?" (Matched emotion, empathy, feel/felt approach, and open-ended question)
>
> *Manuel:* "She's off today. I haven't talked to her yet."
>
> *You:* "Well, do you think that would be a good idea before assuming the worst about her?" (Closed-end, leading to a decision)
>
> *Manuel:* "Yeah, I guess you're right. I'll talk to her first thing tomorrow."
>
> *You:* "Good idea. I'm sure everything will work out fine." (Complimenting decision and reassuring)

In this situation, by using a combination of the strategies and letting Manuel vent, you were able to slowly lower the level of emotion.

Summary

Interpersonal communication is very complex, especially when emotions are involved. The techniques described here can serve as a foundation for improved interactions; however, much practice and effort are required to build effective, straightforward two-way relationships with other people.

References

Blanchard, K., & Johnson, S. (1982). *The one minute manager.* New York: Berkeley Books.

Fullerton, H.N., Jr. (1997, November). Labor force 2006: Slowing down and changing composition. *Monthly Labor Review.* Washington, DC: Bureau of labor Statistics, U.S. Department of Labor, p. 1.

Mehrabian, A. (1968, September). Communicating without words. *Psychology Today, 2,* pp. 52–55.

WORKPLACE SCENARIOS SITUATIONS SHEET

Instructions: Pick one of the scenarios below to play act in your group. One of your group members will play the customer or co-worker so that you can practice responding to an emotional person.

1. You are a call center representative for Holiday Resorts in Daytona Beach, Florida. Your job is to take reservations for your beachfront property over the telephone and to provide customer support for clients who have previously made reservations. You have received a call from a client who is scheduled to check into a condominium tomorrow. Apparently, she has an unexpected work emergency. Her boss has demanded that she cancel her vacation plans and fly to Houston, Texas, tonight or else! She wants to cancel her reservation. The Holiday Resorts policy is that any cancellations (other than for documented personal or family medical emergencies) will result in a forfeiture of 50 percent of the payment. In this case, that amounts to $1,500 dollars.

   Begin your conversation after the caller states her desire to cancel her reservation and says that she wants her money back.

2. You are a teller at Northern Heights Savings and Loan in Chicago, Illinois. A frantic customer has just entered the bank and is waiting in line as several other patrons are served. As he waits, you have noticed him continually fidgeting, glancing around, and looking at his watch. Initially, you were concerned that he might be a robber, but now that he is at your window, you have identified him as a customer. When he stepped up to your window, his voice and words indicated that he was in a hurry. He stated that his car was parked in the disabled space out front, with the motor running, and his wife in labor. He says he tried to withdraw $500 from the ATM machine, but that it was apparently out of order. He also states that he deposited a $5,000 check yesterday. It was given to him as a present for the new baby by his family in Georgia. Upon checking his account record, you realize that without the $5,000, he only has $139.00 in his account. Bank policy is that any check deposited from a out-of-state bank must clear the system before funds are available, and this process takes from five to ten days.

   Begin your part of the conversation after you hear his story and demand for $500 cash from the account which he assumes contains $5,139.

 The 2001 Annual: Volume 1, Training/© 2001 Jossey-Bass/Pfeiffer

3. You are the team leader for the newly established cross-functional marketing team in your organization. The idea of using people from different areas of the organization to develop new strategies for marketing products and services excites you. Your team has met a half dozen times in the past two months. You have known some of the people on the team for a number of years; however, due to the size of your organization, there are members you do not know well. When the team was first formed, meeting rules were established. Additionally, rules for effective brainstorming (see below) were agreed on by everyone. One of the women on the team is from one of your district offices. She has a reputation for being loud, boisterous, and rather demanding when she has an idea. In the middle of your team's brainstorming session, she has proposed an idea and is insisting that it be discussed immediately, although someone has pointed out the brainstorming rule about "No discussion of issues" on the list below:

- No criticism allowed.
- Quantity, not quality, is encouraged.
- Anything goes; all ideas are valid.
- "Piggybacking" of ideas is fine.
- No discussion of issues (this will be done later).
- Everyone participates, no observers.
- One person speaks at a time.
- Use inclusive language (consider diversity).

The woman persists and is becoming very vocal, stressing that her idea using Internet links with partnering companies can add significantly to revenue bases. Although several people have agreed with her, she does not seem satisfied and keeps adding more detail to her idea. Some members of the team are becoming obviously frustrated and irritated.

Begin your part of the conversation at this point.

WORKPLACE SCENARIOS OBSERVATION SHEET

Instructions: In the practice session, the participant who is responding to emotional behavior should use at least two or three of the strategies for dealing with emotional people discussed earlier. Use this sheet to write down your specific observations as the person practices.

1. What did the participant do well? What specific skills did he/she use during this session?

2. What did the person not do well? What mistakes did he/she make that led to an increased emotional state?

3. What suggestions for improvement do you have? What could the person have done differently? Be specific.

674. I Appreciate: Giving Affirmations

Goals

- To learn two stylistic approaches to showing appreciation to others.
- To list some common benefits and barriers to showing appreciation.
- To practice giving appreciation to others.

Group Size

Any size, in subgroups of three.

Time Required

Approximately two hours.

Physical Setting

A room of sufficient size to accommodate a large group discussion. The room may be divided into smaller segments for triad discussions or may have a separate, smaller discussion room nearby.

Materials

- Copies of the I Appreciate Two Approaches to Appreciation background sheet for each participant.
- Copies of the I Appreciate Appreciability Scale for each participant.
- Business size envelopes (one per participant).
- A flip chart and felt-tipped markers.
- Pens or pencils for participants
- Blank paper and a hard surface for writing.

Process

1. Introduce the session by explaining the goals. (Five minutes.)

2. To acquaint participants with what appreciation means, ask participants to think of a time when someone they know voluntarily did something that benefited them in some way.

3. Share a personal experience of feeling appreciation and describe the effects that someone else's voluntary act had on you. (For instance, carrying a heavy box of supplies for a training event across town on a crowded bus and a man offers his seat.) The feelings might be physical relief, reduction in tension about the training program, positive regard for the person, or something else.

4. Ask for three or four volunteers to share their own incidents with the large group. (Ten minutes.)

5. Ask: "Is it hard to show appreciation sometimes? Why do you think this is so?"

6. Ask for volunteers to share their observations and summarize them on the flip chart under "Barriers to Appreciation."(Fifteen minutes.)

7. Give everyone copies of the I Appreciate Two Approaches to Appreciation background sheet and ask participants to read it silently. When everyone has finished, discuss what they have read briefly. (Twenty minutes.)

8. Next give participants copies of the I Appreciate Appreciability Scale and pens or pencils and ask them to complete the scale, score it, and interpret their results. Help participants who may have questions. (Twenty minutes.)

9. Bring the group together and explain that individuals can improve their ability to show appreciation through practice. To give participants an opportunity to express appreciation to someone who has helped them in some way, but to whom they have not expressed appreciation, explain that they will be completing an activity in triads. Divide the group into sets of three. (Five minutes.)

10. Explain that each person is to think of someone who has done something worthy of appreciation, but for whom he or she has found it difficult to give appreciation. Tell them to write down briefly who the person is and what the person did that they appreciate. Emphasize that they should strive for specificity, particularly in how the action taken by the other person helped them and how the act affected them. When individuals have completed their descriptions, they should read them to one another, one at a time, as

other members of the triad listen. Then the two listeners are to share their feelings and thoughts about how the message affected them. After each person has shared his or her descriptions, all participants are to rewrite their descriptions to take account of the feedback from the others. They are to write personal notes to the persons they appreciate.

11. Give participants envelopes in which to place the notes. The envelopes will be given to the people at a later time. Explain that participants can mail or hand the note to a person, but it is preferable to give appreciation orally and face to face. Point out that people make choices to give or not to give appreciation. However, making the choice to give it benefits both the other people and themselves and allows the giver to experience joy that comes with the commitment to learn a new behavior. (Thirty minutes.)

12. Reconvene the large group and ask for comments regarding the activity.

- How did you feel about this activity?

- How did you feel about sharing your description with the others in your group?

- It is easy to appreciate people who have done good things for us. But how can we appreciate the good things in someone whom we may not like? Or who has made a mistake? Or when the person has not communicated with us?

- How can we develop a greater capacity to give and receive appreciation?

- What will you do tomorrow to start practicing this new behavior?

(Fifteen minutes.)

Variation

- Participants may wish to invent a situation in their small groups to role play. They may select one or more of their situations and construct a scenario in which the participant gives his or her appreciation. One of the participants then would play the role of an observer and give feedback on the role play. If individuals select the role-play option, allow extra time (approximately fifteen minutes).

Submitted by A. Carol Rusaw.

A. Carol Rusaw is an associate professor of interpersonal and organizational communication at the University of Louisiana, Lafayette. She has a doctorate in adult education/human resource development and has twenty years' experience in training and consulting. She has written over a dozen journal articles in the field in addition to two books: Transforming the Character of Public Organizations: Techniques for Change Agents *and* Leading Public Organizations: An Interactive Approach.

I Appreciate Two Approaches to Appreciation

To receive appreciation is a special gift, and the ability to give appreciation to others is especially important in interpersonal relationships. For those who have gone out of their way to help us, we give them our thanks. For people who do small things that make life easier, we are grateful. Giving as well as receiving appreciation, however, is not always easy.

We may be reluctant to give people appreciation because we see many negative qualities in the person as well as positive. Further, if we do express thanks, some people do not accept it well or are embarrassed by it. Others may believe that we are trying to manipulate them in some way or are being kind only because that is what is required or socially accepted.

Further, some of us may find it easier or more difficult to give appreciation because of different views we hold of ourselves and of others. Although there are many ways we see ourselves in relation to others, two of the more noteworthy approaches are *narcissistic* and *transpersonal*. They are noteworthy in the sense that they are opposite poles. Most of us have some degree of both characteristics within us.

Narcissistic Views

Narcissistic personalities find it hard to express appreciation spontaneously and genuinely because giving credit to someone else chates their own self esteem. Brown (1997) describes narcissistic personalities as showing strong needs to enhance or protect their egos. Narcissism stems from a state in which individuals act out of desire.

In their quest for pure ego fulfillment, Brown notes, narcissistic personalities have six prominent behaviors:

1. *Denial:* A disclaimer of responsibility for faults. This may lead the narcissistic personality to blame others or external events for problems he or she created.

2. *Rationalization:* An attempt to justify unacceptable behavior or feelings. This produces a personally derived set of criteria on which to evaluate the behaviors of others selectively.

3. *Attributional Egotism:* An attempt to find positive reasons for self-serving behaviors, particularly when those behaviors have benefited others.

4. *Self-Aggrandizement:* Narcissistic individuals lack a distinction between their "ideal" selves and what is "actual." Consequently, they see themselves as

unique—perhaps even superhuman. This may lead them to seek out compliments that boost their high-toned self-images, but ignore or disparage remarks that assail it. People find that narcissists often take sincere compliments "the wrong way."

5. *Belief in Entitlement:* A feeling that one has a "right" to exploit others. This often occurs when narcissists have legal or personal power over others. Those who are indebted to narcissists in some way become their captives.

6. *Anxiety:* Because of their own belief in fear as a motivator, narcissistic personalities become victims of fear themselves. Underlying their abuse of power and control of others is a sense of dejection, hypersensitivity, and worthlessness.

Transpersonal Views

Some individuals show appreciation not so much from desire for material gain, or because they have a legal or moral obligation, or because they fear losing someone else's regard. Rather, their sincerity is based on a transpersonal (or "trans-egotistic") orientation. Transpersonal personalities are non-judgmental: They show a feeling of accepting the other even if the other has many negative characteristics or behaviors. Transpersonal personalities realize a cosmopolitan awareness of qualities that people have in common. Yet, they also realize the importance of individual differences that give people unique identities. Transpersonal personalities use appreciation as a means of validating—and deepening—their regard for others.

Some common transpersonal personality characteristics, based on descriptions in Lajoie and Shapiro (1992), include:

1. *Self-Transcendence:* A belief that the self can expand beyond its immediate cultural contexts and desires. Individuals with transpersonal characteristics define "self" as a unique identity that one learns and practices from various social roles and responsibilities.

2. *Evolution to Highest Potential:* In the process of developing their identities through social learning, people can achieve a unique meaning and relationship within the cosmos. Transpersonals see mistakes they make along the way as potential means of learning and growth.

3. *Process Versus End Result:* Because people are in a continual state of evolution or "becoming," transpersonals cannot see anyone as having attained a perfect existence. The means by which people understand or become aware of this process is a sign of growth.

4. *Holistic View of Reality:* From a transpersonal viewpoint, people realize meaning from "peak experiences," or moments of heightened self-awareness. This occurs during a convergence of physical, mental, emotional, and spiritual states of consciousness.

5. *Respect for Individual Interpretations:* Transpersonal personalities regard the social learning process as one in which individuals define social reality. Each interpretation, accordingly, has merit if it is seen from the person's point of view. The transpersonal set of assumptions is nonjudgmental and accepting.

Conclusion

Each of us has elements of narcissistic as well as transpersonal personality characteristics. The blend of the two varies and depends on circumstances. Knowing the strengths and weaknesses of each type of personality characteristic, however, helps us know when we are ineffective because of the characteristics of one or the other. Through obtaining feedback and practicing giving appreciation to others in particular social situations, we can learn what is effective. Learning to appreciate the gracious acts of others and to show that appreciation take practice.

The differences between how narcissistic and transpersonal personalities see themselves and others and how and why they communicate appreciation can be compared using five descriptors:

1. *External Causality Versus Internal Responsibility:* Narcissistic personalities attribute causes to outside conditions and may be highly selective about to whom and why to give appreciation. Transpersonal personalities see causality as multiple, humanly defined, and open to many possible interpretations. They see gestures of appreciation as spontaneous and a means of self-expression.

2. *Fear/Suspicion Versus Acceptance:* Narcissistic personalities are driven by fear and may easily suspect others of wrongdoing. Transpersonal personalities accept the merits of what others do and show appreciation readily.

3. *Judgment Versus Tolerance:* Narcissistic personalities accept as valid their own criteria to assess the contributions of others. Transpersonal personalities see criteria as based in social norms and behaviors and valid according to the requirements of different situations.

4. *Self-Protection Versus Self-Disclosure:* Narcissistic personalities may use appreciation as a tool for enhancing their own self-images. Transpersonal

personalities believe that sharing feelings, particularly appreciation, builds self-esteem in oneself and others.

5. *Preoccupation with Results Versus Respect for Process:* Narcissistic personalities seek control and establish definitive expectations for how things should occur. Transpersonal personalities, however, focus on the logic people use for solving problems.

References

Brown, A. (1997, July). Narcissism, identity, and legitimacy. *Academy of Management Review, 22*(3), 643–686.

Lajoie, D.H., & Shapiro, S.I. (1992). Definitions of transpersonal psychology: The first twenty-three years. *The Journal of Transpersonal Psychology, 24*(1), 79–98.

I Appreciate Appreciability Scale

The following scale was developed to examine the effects of narcissism and transpersonal characteristics in relation to giving and receiving appreciation. It is based on the assumption that the view of self and others determines how individuals give and receive appreciation. Although we may not have learned to genuinely appreciate every act of kindness others direct toward us, we can improve that frequency through discipline and practice. The scale can be used to develop greater appreciation for what others do for us.

Instructions: The following statements examine some typical responses to giving and receiving appreciation. As you read the items, mark the extent to which you believe they coincide with *your typical responses.* Use a scale of 1 to 5, with 1 being "not at all like me" and 5 being "very much like me." When you have finished, go to the end of the scale and compute your scores following the directions provided.

1 = not at all like me
2 = not too much like me
3 = sometimes like me, sometimes not
4 = much like me
5 = very much like me

_____ 1. I could get more done in my organization if there were less "red tape."

_____ 2. I believe people should be commended for trying, even if they don't succeed.

3. Fear is an important factor in success.

_____ 4. Giving appreciation obligates you.

_____ 5. When I criticize someone, I show respect for the person.

_____ 6. I believe that achievements should be rewarded and mistakes punished.

_____ 7. When someone gives me an explanation that doesn't coincide with my own values and opinions, I usually give the person the benefit of a doubt.

_____ 8. I own up to errors if I make a bad choice.

_____ 9. I appraise someone else's performance based on my own criteria.

_____ 10. I find it easy to share things about myself with others.

_____ 11. I find it difficult to look at new information or ideas after I have formed an opinion.

_____ 12. I do not appreciate people if they fail to meet objective performance standards.

_____ 13. If people make mistakes, I try to understand their reasoning processes.

_____ 14. If people give me compliments, I often wonder, "What's up their sleeves?"

_____ 15. I usually give appreciation by stating how something affected me personally.

_____ 16. People see me as intimidating.

_____ 17. I tend to see the whole picture when I appraise someone's actions.

_____ 18. I have a need to be right most of the time.

_____ 19. I find small things for which to praise people.

_____ 20. When someone questions my actions, I put a "positive spin" on what I did.

_____ 21. When people do something nice for me, I know they mean it sincerely.

_____ 22. If people make mistakes, they should be required to justify them.

_____ 23. I understand when someone from a different culture is being kind to me.

_____ 24. I carry a "chip" on my shoulder if someone criticizes me unfairly.

_____ 25. If someone is praised for an action, I feel that he or she really earned it.

Scoring

Instructions: To score your results, mark the items for which you answered either a "4" or a "5" and write ONLY those scores in the blanks below. *Do not write in scores for "3" and below.*

Add the number of entries for each column. For Column A, multiply the number by 4 and divide by 39. Then multiply by 100 to obtain a percentage. This is your Narcissism score. For Column B, multiply the number by 2 and divide by 24. Then multiply by 100 to obtain a percentage. This is your Transpersonal score. The higher the percentage, the greater the extent of either narcissism or transpersonal personality characteristics you have. If your score in both columns is low, it indicates you have a capacity for learning and can adapt fairly easily to different situational requirements.

Column A   **Column B**

Item: Item:

1. _____   2. _____

3. _____   5. _____

4. _____   7. _____

6. _____   8. _____

9. _____   10. _____

11.   13. _____

12. _____   15. _____

14. _____   17. _____

16. _____   19. _____

18. _____   21. _____

20. _____   23. _____

22. _____   25. _____

24. _____

Number of "4's" and "5's" in Column A _____ x 4

Number of "4's" and "5's" in Column B _____ x 2

Total Column A: _____ /39 = _____ x 100 = _____

Total Column B: _____ /24 = _____ x 100 = _____

Narcissism Score (A): _____ %   Transpersonal Score (B): _____ %

675. New Owners:
Planning Organizational Action

Goals

- To provide participants the opportunity to examine their organization as though they were the owners with ultimate accountability for outcomes.

- To provide a forum for participants to suggest, discuss, and decide on practical courses of action to improve organizational efficiency.

- To give participants the opportunity to participate in a collaborative group process.

Group Size

Any number of participants from the same organization, in subgroups of four to seven.

Time Required

Approximately two to three hours, depending on the number of subgroups.

Materials

- A New Owners Group Task Sheet for each participant, prepared by the facilitator in advance to be specific to the organization and work teams.

- Newsprint and felt-tipped markers for each subgroup.

- Paper and pencils for each participant.

Physical Setting

A room with movable chairs in which participants can meet in small groups. Round tables to write on are preferable.

Process

1. Explain that in our competitive environment it is necessary to remain continually alert for ways to improve organizational effectiveness. Say that organizations that provide the best services and products are those in which members feel a strong level of accountability and commitment, in which ideas are generated and discussed by everyone involved, and in which action plans are generated and implemented. (Three to five minutes.)

2. Tell the participants that they will now have the opportunity to practice these behaviors in a very lifelike setting: Their own organization. Form heterogeneous groups of four to seven participants, preferably with individuals from various parts of the organization to obtain a more diverse point of view. (Three to five minutes.)

3. Distribute the New Owners Group Task Sheet and a pencil to each individual and describe the process. Clarify any questions and instruct the groups to begin their task. Tell them they will have approximately one hour. (Three to five minutes.)

4. As the groups complete their tasks, reach conclusions, and list them on newsprint for later presentation to the large group, go from group to group, being sure they are on task and answering any questions. (Sixty minutes.)

5. Reassemble the large group and ask a spokesperson from each subgroup to present the results in the form of an action plan for (a) the first month, (b) the first six months, (c) the first year, and (d) beyond. Encourage members of other subgroups to question, challenge, and clarify other plans.

6. After the subgroups have completed their presentations, explain that this need not be just a training exercise, as many of the plans have real merit for improving the current organization. Go over each subgroup's results in the large group again to find specific actions that could actually be implemented at this time to improve the organization's effectiveness. List these ideas on newsprint.

7. Help the large group prioritize the list of items. Assign people to be in charge of integrating the actions rated with the highest priority into the organization's existing plans. List the person responsible, the expected outcome, and the anticipated completion date beside each item on a new sheet of flip-chart paper. (Sixty to ninety minutes.)

8. Ask the group:

- What have you learned from this experience?
- How will you integrate what you have learned into your work on a daily basis?
- What advice do you have to give organizational leaders?

Variations

- The New Owners Group Task Sheet can be developed so that only a portion of the organization, such as specific services or specific products, are taken over by the groups. Various groups need not have the same service or product as their task. The whole organization can be divided, and the different pieces can be sold to different groups.

- Not-for-profit organizations can be the subject of the activity, with the participants serving as the organization's newly appointed board of directors.

- The process of creating priorities might be done through the Nominal Group Technique (Ford, Delbecq, & Van de Ven, 1975, p. 35) or a modified Delphi Technique (Bunning, 1979, p. 174).

- The process can be merged with an annual planning process such as Management by Objectives (Thomson, 1972, p. 130).

- You may wish to have the participants examine, receive feedback, and discuss their own behaviors in the leaderless group decision process that they have just completed.

- A senior person such as the plant manager or president may be invited to attend the final portion of the process to receive suggestions, approve implementation where feasible, and provide feedback for suggestions that are not feasible.

References

Bunning, R.L. (1979). The Delphi technique. In J.E. Jones & J.W. Pfeiffer (Eds.), *The 1979 annual handbook for group facilitators*. San Francisco, CA: Jossey-Bass/Pfeiffer.

Ford, D.L., Jr., Delbecq, A., & Van de Ven, A. (1975). Nominal group technique: An applied group problem-solving activity. In J.E. Jones & J.W. Pfeiffer (Eds.), *The 1975 annual handbook for group facilitators*. San Francisco, CA: Jossey-Bass/Pfeiffer.

Thomson, T.M. (1972). Management by objectives. In J.W. Pfeiffer & J.E. Jones (Eds.), *The 1972 annual handbook for group facilitators.* San Francisco, CA: Jossey-Bass/Pfeiffer.

―――――――

Submitted by Richard L. Bunning.

Richard L. Bunning *has more than twenty-five years of experience in personnel, organization development, and training. He holds a Ph.D. from Arizona State University and is currently a European-based partner with Phoenix Associates, an organization development consulting firm. He has practiced as a management consultant in Europe since 1991 and has published more than thirty practitioner-oriented articles in a variety of management and personnel journals and publications.*

NEW OWNERS GROUP TASK SHEET

The Situation

Our organization has made a decision to discontinue [choose a specific service/process/product/engaging in the business altogether]. There will, however, continue to be a market for this service/product through another organization and/or the same customers as before.

Negotiations are in process to sell this portion of the business to a group of current employees, who are sitting here now. Your group has formed a partnership arrangement, with each person having equal voting rights and all sharing equally in profits. Each of you has come up with enough money to invest equally in this offshoot from the current business. That money, your life savings, has been pooled to provide the capital necessary to purchase the organization and retain some initial operating capital.

In addition, you have obtained contracts to continue to supply [above mentioned service or product] at a rate equal to what is now being provided. Costs will be equal, with the exception of the current management's salary and any other overhead charges that would no longer apply.

The Task

Your group will take over ownership of the organization two weeks from today. As a new, small, privately owned organization, you are free to make changes (even radical changes) in procedures, personnel, policies, wages, benefits, etc. Your task is to discuss such changes and develop an action plan for what you want to accomplish:

- The first week
- The first month
- The first six months
- The first year
- Longer term

List your plans for your new organization on newsprint and choose a spokesperson who will present and justify your plans to the large group. You have sixty minutes to complete this task.

676. Logos: Taking Pride in Team Products

Goals

- To help members of a new team become acquainted through sharing personal information.
- To develop a team through creating and producing a product.
- To create a team identity and sense of pride.

Group Size

As many as twenty participants, in newly formed teams within an organization.

Time Required

Approximately two hours.

Materials

- One copy of the Logos Team Development Worksheet for each participant.
- Newsprint and an easel for each team.
- Felt-tipped markers for each team.
- Pencils and paper for participants.

Physical Setting

A room large enough to accommodate four working groups of five members each.

Process

1. Share the goals of the activity and hand out a copy of the Logos Team Development Worksheet, extra paper, and a pencil to each participant.

2. Instruct the participants to form into their work teams and to share at least three quick bits of personal information to warm up if they do not know one another well. (Three minutes.)

3. Tell the teams to choose a leader, a recorder, and a spokesperson for the team.

4. Tell participants to first work alone to complete the information on the Logos Team Development Worksheet. (Ten minutes.)

5. Tell the teams that each person should share his or her information before group discussion of the task begins. (Fifteen minutes.)

6. After each team has collected data from each of the team members, instruct the teams to work on a project that will include the following tasks, which you have printed on a flip chart. (Thirty minutes.)

   ■ Create a visual aid with a team logo.

   ■ The logo should describe your team's "strengths" and "abilities."

   ■ The logo should also include your team's values.

   ■ Include one word that best defines your team.

   ■ Use all of your team members to create a three-minute presentation to share your logo information with the whole group.

7. Ask each team, in turn, to present its logo and other information to the entire group.

8. Lead a discussion with the whole group using the following questions:

   ■ What are your reactions to this experience?

   ■ What observations can you share about your team process?

   ■ How was this activity similar to or different from working on a project back at work?

   ■ What produced good teamwork? What hindered your teamwork?

   ■ What generalizations can be made about work teams and project development?

   ■ How will you apply the principles you have learned at your work site?

Submitted by Bonnie Jameson.

Bonnie Jameson is a designer, trainer, and facilitator in all areas of human resource development and organization development. She is an associate professor at California State University at Hayward, California, where she designs and teaches courses in the Nonprofit Management Program and the Training for Trainers Certificate Program. Ms. Jameson consults with schools, nonprofit organizations, and businesses. Ten of Ms. Jameson's structured experiences have been published in the Jossey-Bass/Pfeiffer Annuals. *She co-authored* Inspiring Fabled Service *(Jossey-Bass, 1996) with Betsy Sanders.*

LOGOS TEAM DEVELOPMENT WORKSHEET

Instructions: Write at least three items about yourself under each of the headings below. Then think of one word that describes you in a nutshell and list it also. You will have ten minutes to complete the worksheet.

Strengths That You Bring to the Team:

Abilities You Bring to the Team:

Your Most Important Values:

One-Word Description of You:

677. When Shall We Meet Again?
Assessing Information in Teams

Goals

- To demonstrate how teams assess information to make a decision.

- To develop participant awareness of the group's process for evaluating information.

- To demonstrate the importance of having a process to make a decision.

- To show the emergence of leadership in a new team.

Group Size

Any number over five to as many as the room can hold or the number of information cards you have prepared. The activity is especially well-suited for a newly formed team of any type.

Time Required

Thirty to forty-five minutes.

Materials

- A prepared flip chart with the following question written legibly: "Given the information you have received by e-mail (on the index cards), when will your team meet next week (day and time)?"

- Prepared e-mail/index cards. Each index card should have one of the following pieces of information neatly printed:

  - The team agreed that Mondays are a bad time to meet because everyone's just returning from the weekend and preparing for the work week.

  - Mary usually takes the minutes.

- Many people in the office go bowling on Thursday nights.

- The coffee machine is three doors down from the conference room.

- The conference room has an oval table with ten chairs around it.

- John and Kathy always arrive at work by 6:30 a.m.

- A flip chart and markers are in the conference room.

- Sally and Roger have to leave work by 4:00 p.m.

- The team agreed that Fridays are a bad time to meet. Everybody's preparing to leave for the weekend (if they haven't already left).

- The company has 211 employees.

- Kristin is the team leader.

- Treena thinks that team meetings are usually a waste of time.

- Ken has been looking forward to the team meeting. He has a very important issue he'd like to raise.

- The overhead projector light bulb is burned out.

- There isn't a whiteboard in the conference room.

- The team agreed that the team leader prepares the agenda and leads the meeting.

- Kristin is going to be out of town on Tuesday and Wednesday.

- The conference room is booked on Thursday from 8 a.m. to 12 noon.

- The conference room is booked on Wednesday from 8 a.m. to 12 noon.

Note: If the group is exceptionally large, or you want to add to the confusion, you may add your own irrelevant information cards.

Physical Setting

A room large enough to have all the participants within view of one another.

Process

1. Invite the group to participate in a team activity that will give them a glimpse into their group dynamics. Tell the group: "Your team needs to meet for four hours next week. You have been exchanging e-mails to determine the best day and time to meet. Your e-mail exchanges are written on these index cards."

2. Mix up the cards and give at least one card to each team member. Remind them that their task is to answer the question written on the flip chart. Then stand out of the way and watch the team dynamics!

3. As the team attempts to solve the riddle, you may witness some common traps. Write the traps below on a flip chart (out of view of participants) for later discussion:

   - *No Process.* The team just starts shouting out the information they have on the cards, without planning how to handle the task.

   - *Process Loss.* The team ignores someone who has the answer (or something close to it).

   - *Hero Emerges.* One person solves the riddle and declares victory, while making his/her teammates feel left out or stupid.

   - *Poor Communication Skills.* Talking over each other, interrupting, dominating the conversation.

   - *Assumptions.* The team begins to make assumptions about which information is relevant and which is not without any criteria to assess it.

   - *Agonizing About the Irrelevant.* Just in case they miss something, the team goes over each piece of information.

   - *Paranoia.* Could it be a trap? Could it be one of those team activities that "get you" in the end? Is there something the facilitator just isn't telling us?

4. Just be patient, allowing about fifteen minutes for the process to evolve. Take notes for the debriefing. Eventually, the team should figure out the need for structure and a process. One person will take the "leadership role," define a process, and lead the team to the logical conclusion. (Fifteen minutes.)

5. The answer is deceptively simple: The team must meet on Thursday from 12 noon until 4 p.m. The team has agreed it cannot meet on Mondays and Fridays. Kristin has to be at the meeting, and she'll be out of town on Tuesday and Wednesday. The conference room is booked on Thursday from 8 a.m. to 12 noon.

6. Stop the group and show them the list of common traps you made on the flip chart. Ask whether they fell into any of these traps and why. Have them discuss ways to avoid these pitfalls in the future and make a list on the flip chart for them to use at their next group meeting. (Ten minutes.)

7. Debrief the activity, using some of the following questions:

- What worked well?

- What could the group have done better?

- How might the team work better together in the future?

- Who emerged as a leader and why? What qualities did this person possess?

- What process might be used the next time the team must assess information? How could you be sure to remember to use the process in the future?

(Ten minutes.)

Submitted by Kristin J. Arnold.

Kristin J. Arnold, CPCM, specializes in facilitating leadership, management, and employee teams, particularly in the areas of strategic planning, process improvement, decision making, and collaborative problem solving. An author, national speaker, and featured columnist in The Daily Press, *Ms. Arnold is regarded as an expert in team development. With building extraordinary teams as her signature service, she has provided process facilitation, training, and coaching support to both public- and private-sector initiatives.*

678. Risk Tolerance: Understanding the Utility of Taking Risks

Goals

- To explore and understand risk as it relates to planning and decision making.

- To demonstrate the duality of risk.

- To enable risk-aversive participants to explore their negative bias toward risk.

- To demonstrate how a long-term view of risk can create short-term risk tolerance.

- To demonstrate that investments and loans can be used to express and manage risk. (Requires use of advanced rules and questions presented in the Variations section.)

Group Size

Any size group divided into subgroups of four to six.

Time Required

Forty-five minutes for five rounds, although it is possible to use only three rounds and cut off about ten minutes.

Materials

- One Risk Tolerance Constraints Sheet per participant.

- One Risk Tolerance Score Sheet per subgroup.

- Pencils for all participants.

- Stop watch.

- A flip chart and felt-tipped markers.

- (Optional) A visual display of the Score Sheet, either on an overhead transparency or flip-chart sheet.

- (Optional) A visual display of the game parameters for group referral.

Physical Setting

A room large enough to allow subgroups to discuss strategy without being overheard by other subgroups.

Process

1. Explain that the activity is about tolerance for risk. Say that participants are to think of themselves as members of small "companies" and that each "company" will have a simple goal—"Minimize cost, maximize profit"— as they go through several rounds of the activity.

2. Form the participants into subgroups of four to six members each and have each subgroup sit well apart from other subgroups.

3. Say to the group: "In the next ten minutes, your task is to develop a strategy that—after five rounds of play—will best meet the goal of minimizing cost and maximizing profit while operating under the constraints on the Risk Tolerance Constraints Sheet." Hand out copies of the Constraints Sheet (or project it onto a screen, if desired) and pencils. Read the constraints as everyone follows along.

4. Ask whether there are any questions. Once the questions have been asked and answered, begin the activity by handing out a Risk Tolerance Score Sheet to each subgroup and telling all groups to record the choices they plan to make for that round on their Score Sheets. Explain that they will be able to change their choices at the beginning of each round. Tell the groups to begin, reminding them that they will have ten minutes to develop a plan and write it on their Score Sheets. (You may want to have the subgroups post their plans on a sheet of newsprint so that changes can be verified more easily.) (Ten minutes.)

5. After all the subgroups have completed and posted their plans, conduct five rounds in this manner:

   - Ask whether any groups want to amend their plans. If one does, allow two minutes for them to do so. Then have the groups assess and record earnings or losses related to their decision to maintain or amend their plans.

- Ask the groups to report their costs, that is, expenditures for letters and insurance purchased. Have the groups record that information on their Score Sheets.

- Toss a coin and report the results. Have each group report its profits or losses and post them on their Score Sheets.

6. After five rounds, declare the winner and present an award, if desired.

7. Bring closure to the activity with the following discussion questions:

- Was the dual goal of minimizing cost and maximizing profit realistic? (Help participants see that the most profit was not generated by the least cost, so minimizing cost will not necessarily yield maximum profit.)

- What is the relationship between cost and risk? (Cost is monetarily expressed risk.)

- Which was the riskier choice, A or B? Why? (B was the riskier choice, both in terms of potential gain and in terms of potential loss.)

- Can you see the duality of risk as we look at B? How was risk both positive and negative in terms of potential consequences?

- Why is there a natural propensity to view risk as something to be avoided, and thus to be risk aversive? (A focus on negative consequences can lead to risk aversion.)

- What was the relationship of insurance to risk? How did it affect attitude toward risk in your group? What kinds of "insurance" cannot be purchased but are available to us in our daily lives and business?

- Was it realistic or appropriate for a change in plans to be penalized? Why or why not? (Change incurs additional costs.)

- How did the long-term planning—five rounds—affect risk taking? How can this apply to our own planning, personally or organizationally, in terms of taking risk-tolerant or risk-averse positions?

- What role did trust play in this activity? How was this trust expressed? In whom? In what?

Variations

- If time permits, have participants share their plans prior to the closure questions using this format:

  1. Plan (Strategy regarding cost minimization, maximizing profit, and risk)

2. Execution of the Plan. Were changes made to the plan? Why or why not?

3. At Least Three Lessons Learned

- The activity can be used to bring out the added dimensions of risk by add-ing these two rules:

  1. You will earn 10 percent interest each round on any uncommitted money remaining after you have purchased your letters and insur-ance, but before profits or losses have been determined.

  2. You can take out loans each round for up to 50 percent of the cash that is available at the beginning of each round. You must pay back the accumulated principle by Round 4 or pay a penalty of accumu-lated principle, plus 20 percent at the end of Round 5.

- If these rules are added, use these additional discussion questions:

  1. How did the use of loans affect risk taking?

  2. How can the idea of loans be transferred to taking risk in general? In other words, what are some emotional or operational "loans" that it is possible to take? What can we say about propensity for taking risk among those who take such "loans"?

  3. Why was a change in the plan penalized? (Adjusting to change has as-sociated costs.)

  4. What does the use of interest and loans tell us about long-term views of risk? How can we relate this to strategic planning and development? (A long-term view of risk may enable people to take riskier positions for the short term.)

- You may explore how complex verbal rules can affect decisions, for example, how complex rules can cause erroneous assumptions and misconceptions.

Submitted by Edward Earl Hampton, Jr.

Edward Earl Hampton, Jr., president of Performance Perspectives and vice pres-ident for MAREDAH, Inc., is an organization development consultant and coach who specializes in organization development, leadership coaching, organizational troubleshooting, change management, and training on a wide range of manage-ment and leadership topics. He teaches leadership and management topics as part of the faculty for the Industrial Engineering and Management Sciences Depart-ment at the University of Central Florida in Orlando, Florida.

RISK TOLERANCE CONSTRAINTS SHEET

Starting capital: $1,000

Instructions: Each round you will purchase A's or B's. You may choose a mix of A's and B's, and you may choose more than one A or more than one B per round. Some time during the round, after you have made your letter selection, "fate" will choose an X or Y by flipping a coin. Heads will result in an X, tails in a Y. You will be paid according to the combinations that result from the choices made by you and by fate, as explained below.

- Each B costs $100; each A costs $50.
- Each AX combination results in $100 profit to your company.
- Each BX combination results in $300 profit to your company.
- Each AY combination results in a loss of $200 to your company.
- Each BY combination results in a loss of $500 to your company.
- For each round that you execute your plan without making any changes, you will earn $100 as a bonus.
- For each round that you change your plan, you will be penalized $200.
- Insurance is available at $25 per letter per round. Insurance guarantees $50 in profit if fate deals a Y.

We will determine the cost and profit for each round in this way:

- Prior to fate casting its decision, you will record your costs incurred for that round (letter A or letter B, plus insurance purchases).
- Once fate has cast its lot, you will then determine the profit or loss incurred for that round and record it on the Score Sheet.

After all five rounds are completed, we will compare the costs and profits generated by each group over the five rounds. The group with the most profit at minimum cost will be the winner.

Earned Interest (Optional)

- Uncommitted capital earns compound interest of 10 percent for each round.

Loans (Optional)

- Balloon payment of outstanding principle plus 20 percent is due at the end of Round 5.

- Loans are capped at 50 percent of cash on hand at beginning of the round being played.

- No interest is collected if principle is paid by the end of Round 4.

Risk Tolerance Score Sheet

Round	C	P	C	P	C	P	C	P
1								
2								
3								
4								
5								
Totals								

C = Cost
P = Profit

679. Nicknames: Summarizing What You Hear

Goals

- To develop skills in creative thinking and active listening.
- To generate performance feedback in an established group through the use of nicknames.
- To receive feedback on how participants perceive one another.

Group Size

Any number of established groups, with three to six members each or a larger intact group that can be divided into subgroups of three to six.

Time Required

Approximately ninety minutes.

Materials

- A Nicknames Worksheet for every participant.
- Pencils for all participants.
- Masking tape.
- A flip chart and felt-tipped markers.

Physical Setting

A room large enough for individuals to complete their worksheets in private and for groups to meet and discuss their completed forms. Moveable desks or chairs are required.

Process

1. Have participants form into their normal work teams or divide a larger intact group into subgroups of three to six members each. Inform participants

that they are about to engage in a listening skill development exercise that will help their teams.

2. Distribute Nicknames Worksheets and pencils to all participants and explain the layout of the worksheet. (Five minutes.)

3. Instruct individuals to list the names of the team members sitting with them in the left column. In the middle column, labeled "Nickname," ask them to select and write an appropriate nickname for each person, based on the person's behavior in past group activities. Give everyone a few minutes to come up with nicknames and write them down. (Ten minutes.)

4. In the last column, "Reasons," have participants provide brief details about why they chose each particular nickname. (Ten minutes.)

5. Have everyone fill in the bottom of the form with their own names and nicknames for themselves.

6. When all worksheets are complete, have each team form a circle and prepare to share the nicknames they created for others. Select a member at random to begin the process of sharing by first telling everyone the nickname he or she selected for himself or herself and the reasons for the choice, then listening as the others give the nicknames they have chosen for him or her and the reasons for their choices. Each person is to listen closely and then summarize in one sentence what he or she has heard from the other group members.

7. Continue around the circle with this process until everyone has shared the nicknames they selected for themselves, listened to nicknames chosen by others, and summarized what they have heard about themselves in one sentence. (Twenty to thirty minutes.)

8. Ask each team for a sample of its nicknames and write them on a flip chart. Ask whether there were surprises about the nicknames selected, and solicit reasons given for the nicknames. Ask each group to explore the following questions:

   ■ How would you summarize the characteristics of your team as a whole?

   ■ What impact does that have on how you work together?

   ■ How well did your team members listen to what others were saying about them?

   ■ What characteristics and qualities are present in your group, as evidenced by the nicknames you gave one another?

   ■ What can you do in the future to be more efficient and effective as a team, based on what you have learned about one another?

   (Ten minutes.)

9. Circulate among the subgroups and prompt them, if necessary, to fully discuss any implications that their nicknames and previous sharing have for the way they will work together in the future. (Ten minutes.)

10. Ask the subgroups to take turns and report back to the large group on implications of this activity. Point out any instances of giving good feedback to one another and remind the groups of whatever stage of development they may be in. (Fifteen minutes.)

Variations

- Instead of assigning nicknames to team members, groups can discuss and give names to other teams with whom they work.

- Nicknames can be created but not shared. A list of nicknames can be posted and the team members can try to guess which people were given which nicknames, by whom, and why. The large group could use this matching variation if the members know one another reasonably well.

- Ask the large group to assign nicknames to individuals, then award prizes for the most unusual, most fitting, or funniest nicknames through voting or consensus. (This activity could become a decision-making task at this point.)

- After the activity, the large group can discuss the impact that nicknames have on team and individual development, for example, how it can help and hinder group development.

Submitted by Michael P. Bochenek.

Michael P. Bochenek, Ph.D., is an assistant professor of business administration at Elmhurst College in Elmhurst, Illinois. Previously, he worked for twenty-five years in staffing, training, compensation, equal opportunity, and labor relations at AT&T, where he first utilized experiential activities in employee-development workshops. His work has been published in the 1998 and 1999 Annuals, the 1999 and 2000 McGraw-Hill Sourcebooks, the Management Development Forum, and the International Journal of Conflict Management. He received his Ph.D. in sociology from Loyola University in Chicago.

NICKNAMES WORKSHEET

Person	Nickname	Reason
Your Name		

680. Age Barometer: Energizing a Group

Goals

- To open discussion among participants at the beginning of a workshop or meeting.
- To lighten the mood of a group at any time when energy is low.
- To provide an energizer or way to become acquainted.

Group Size

Any number of participants.

Time Required

Forty minutes.

Materials

- Handout or overhead transparency of an Age Barometer Listing, prepared in advance from the Age Barometer Sample Listing.

Physical Setting

Any room in which small groups can meet comfortably.

Process

1. Prior to using this activity, review the Age Barometer Sample Listing and add items that might be more appropriate for your group or take those off that would have no meaning for your participants. See the following list of categories for some ideas:

   Automobiles (Edsel, Hudson, Maxwell)

Clothing (bell-bottoms, bobby socks, day-glo colors, poodle skirts)

Fads (pinstriping cars, lovers' lanes, listening to Fibber McGee and Molly)

Food (fondue)

Games (Pac Man, pinochle)

Hair styles (bubble cut, flat top)

Hobbies (model building)

Restaurant chains (Bob's Big Boy, Shoney's)

Sports (rollerblading, hang gliding)

Toys (in-line skates vs. fasten-on skates)

2. Prepare a handout or overhead transparency of your own list and have it ready to use at low energy points during a workshop, such as after lunch or after a particularly difficult discussion. It can also be used at the beginning of a workshop as an icebreaker.

3. Give everyone a copy of the handout as they enter the room at the beginning or after a break or project it on the wall so that it can be seen by everyone as they come into the room.

4. When everyone is seated, say to the group: "Let's take a few minutes to get to know each other better, using the sheet of paper in your hand (or the list projected on the wall). Take a pen or pencil and check off all the items you remember well or that have had some impact on your life. If you don't know what an item is, don't check it."

5. When everyone in the group seems to be finished, ask them to form small discussion groups and reminisce about the items, explaining to others what they are, if necessary. (Ten minutes.)

6. Usually the participants will naturally begin to talk about the part that various items have played in their lives without being lead into it. After a few minutes, ask for people to pick one item that has particular meaning for them and to share it within their subgroups. (Ten minutes.)

7. Bring the whole group back together and ask people to introduce themselves or each other to the total group on the basis of the one item they picked. (Fifteen minutes.)

Variation

- An option would be to discuss how what people discovered about one another may affect the outcome of the workshop itself.

Submitted by Robert Alan Black.

Robert Alan Black, Ph.D., founder of Cre8ng People, Places & Possibilities, is a creative thinking consultant and professional speaker who specializes in the S.P.R.E.A.D.ng™ of Creative Thinking throughout workplaces worldwide. During over thirty-five years of creative work, Dr. Black has been a licensed architect, graphics & signage designer, interior designer, tv-news writer and editor, freelance cartoonist, freelance writer, college art professor, and creative thinking and leadership consultant. In addition to being a consultant, he serves as an adjunct professor at Columbus State University in Columbus, Georgia. He is a member of the National Speakers Association, Georgia Speakers Association, American Creativity Association, Creative Education Foundation, National Storytelling Association, and the Southern Order of Storytellers

Age Barometer Sample Listing*

Instructions: Check items on the list below that you remember personally, not just those you may have heard about from others or seen in a movie.

——— 45 RPM records

——— B.F. Flyers

——— Beanie and Cecil

——— Blackjack chewing gum

——— Blue flashbulbs

——— Butch wax™

——— Candy cigarettes

——— Cartoons at Saturday matinees

——— Coffee shops with tableside jukeboxes

——— Cork popguns

——— Drive-ins

——— Hi-fi's

——— Home milk delivery in glass bottles with cardboard stoppers

——— Howdy Doody™

——— Metal ice trays with levers

——— Mimeograph paper

——— Newsreels before the movie

——— Party lines

——— Pea shooters

——— Rollerskate keys

——— S&H Green Stamps

——— Soda machines that dispensed bottles

——— Studebakers or Hudsons

——— Telephone numbers with a word prefix (Olive-6933)

——— Washtub wringers

——— Wax soda pop-shaped bottles with colored sugar water

---

*This list came from the Internet. You may choose to use it as is or create your own list, depending on the group with which you are dealing.

681. TRADE FAIR: DESIGNING JOB AIDS

Goals

- To emphasize and reinforce learning of procedures and system operations.
- To allow participants to learn a procedure in detail and remember its meaning.
- To have a concrete method to check a group's understanding of a procedure.
- To allow participants to customize and adapt procedures to their particular job functions.
- To provide a job aid for participants.

Group Size

Two to twenty participants who are learning a particular procedure for application on the job.

Time Required

Sixty minutes, in addition to time spent learning the material itself.

Materials

- One copy of the Trade Fair Job Aids Design Tips for each participant.
- Sheets of 8½- x 11-inch index paper or small posters for each participant.
- Felt-tipped markers and pencils or pens for preparing the job aids.
- Content-related materials and resources.
- Sticky note pads for each participant.
- Scratch paper for participants.
- Masking tape.

Physical Setting

A room large enough for everyone to walk around and inspect one another's job aids laid out on tables or posted on the wall. In addition to display space, there should be sufficient desk or table space for participants to design their job aids using notes and materials.

Process

1. Announce that after the material to be learned has been presented, the participants will create their own job aids to help them remember the procedure back on the job. Explain that their job aids should reflect a step-by-step process or procedure, so they will want to take excellent notes. Say that job aids should also reflect ways in which the content they learn will affect their jobs. Tell them that they will share their job aids with the entire group at a "Job Aid Trade Fair." (Five minutes.)

2. Deliver the content of the workshop, whether about procedure, policy, or operations. While doing so, remind the participants occasionally that they will be making their own job aids to help them back on the job. Don't cover more points than can be digested easily, and only cover one complete process at a time.

3. After you have finished presenting the material, hand out scratch paper, sticky notes, markers, index stock, markers, and pens or pencils. Tell participants that they will have fifteen minutes to design a job aid based on the procedure they have just learned and another fifteen minutes to actually create it. (More or less time can be allowed, based on the difficulty of the material.)

4. Say to the group:

   "Design your job aid with these specific points in mind: (1) What do you need to know? (2) How will you use it? (3) What decisions will you need to make? (4) What resources or inputs will you need from others?"

5. Distribute the Trade Fair Job Aids Design Tips to the participants.

6. Direct participants to design their job aids first and then to make the job aid as soon as they are ready. Answer questions as necessary. (Fifteen minutes.)

7. Announce the beginning of the production phase in case anyone has not begun to make the actual job aid. Circulate throughout the room and give suggestions or corrections as needed. (Fifteen minutes.)

8. At the end of the time period, announce that the Job Aid Trade Fair will begin. Have everyone either post his or her job aid on the wall with masking tape or leave it on the table. Encourage participants to circulate around the room to examine the other job aids. Provide feedback and praise everyone's efforts. (Ten minutes.)

9. Conduct a discussion or debriefing of the activity, covering points such as:

   ■ The difficulty of the task;

   ■ Whether teams could have been assigned the task rather than individuals; and

   ■ Ways to combine ideas to create better job aids.

10. Give everyone time to make changes to their own job aids if desired and then wrap up the session. (Ten minutes.)

Variations

■ This activity can be adapted to a wide variety of content.

■ Participants may prepare job aids in groups if all members are affected in a similar way. Avoid large, unmanageable groups by dividing participants into smaller teams.

■ If the training class meets on a periodic basis, segment the content so a job aid can be constructed for each installment.

■ If space and time do not allow everyone to circulate around the room, have the participants share what they have done with their immediate neighbors.

■ Awards can be given for the best job aid, in the instructor's opinion, or based on a vote.

Submitted by W. Norman Gustafson

W. Norman Gustafson, M.S., is a trainer, consultant, and educator. He has taught business at the college and high school level for fifteen years. He specializes in performance improvement and new venture planning. His professional interests include e-commerce, marketing strategy, and the application of systems theory to organizational improvement and increased firm value. He participates in Lakewood Research's annual survey of trainers and has previously contributed to the Annual.

TRADE FAIR JOB AIDS DESIGN TIPS

The following tips for creating job aids are taken from the field of process management.

Every process has a *starting point* or state and an *ending point* or desired *state*. A certain number of inputs, steps, decisions, tasks, or transformations result in the desired end state(s). Other states along the way (especially "failure modes") represent a diversion from the path toward the desired outcomes, as shown below.

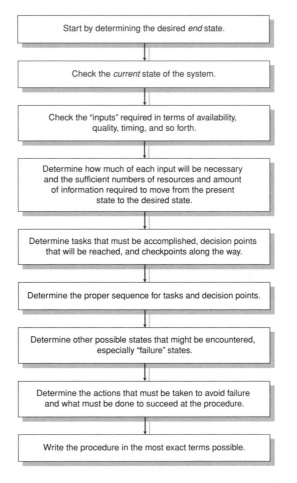

Start by determining the desired *end* state.

Check the *current* state of the system.

Check the "inputs" required in terms of availability, quality, timing, and so forth.

Determine how much of each input will be necessary and the sufficient numbers of resources and amount of information required to move from the present state to the desired state.

Determine tasks that must be accomplished, decision points that will be reached, and checkpoints along the way.

Determine the proper sequence for tasks and decision points.

Determine other possible states that might be encountered, especially "failure" states.

Determine the actions that must be taken to avoid failure and what must be done to succeed at the procedure.

Write the procedure in the most exact terms possible.

682. Show and Tell: Learning About Leadership

Goals

- To focus group participants on the qualities of leadership shown by selected leaders (real or fictional).

- To highlight the leadership skills participants want to demonstrate or use themselves on the job.

- To remind participants of leadership skills they have learned to use when they are back on the job.

Group Size

Up to twenty participants who are attending a workshop on leadership skills.

Time Required

Approximately thirty minutes at the beginning of a workshop, plus another thirty minutes at the end of a workshop.

Materials

- Prior to the actual workshop, participants are told to bring a picture, drawing, sketch, or symbol to use as a reference for a leader they admire. The leader can be real (FDR, JFK, Caesar, Queen Victoria, Wellington, Charles Dickens, Mark Twain, a neighbor or minister) or fictitious (Charlie Brown, Hagar the Horrible, Bugs Bunny, Captain James Kirk, Commander Jean-Luc Picard).

- One flip-chart sheet per participant.

- Two different colored markers per person (preferably washable markers in dark colors).

- A roll of masking tape and scissors for each table.

- Enough wall space for participants to tape up their flip-chart sheets.

Physical Setting

Any training room in which participants can be seated comfortably at tables without the subgroups disturbing one another.

Process

1. This activity can be used at the beginning of a workshop session on leadership, after any opening exercises, introductions, scheduling, or ground rules are given to the participants.

2. Provide markers, masking tape, and flip-chart sheets to all participants.

3. Tell participants to (without consulting with any other participants) tape the picture, sketch, drawing, or symbol or the model leader they brought to the meeting at the top center of their flip-chart sheet under the heading: "My Favorite Leader and Leadership Skills." This should use up no more than the top 20 percent of the sheet.

4. Tell them to draw one horizontal line under the picture, covering the entire width of the sheet from left to right, and to use the same marker to draw a vertical line from the *center* of the horizontal line they've just drawn to the bottom of the flip-chart sheet.

5. Tell participants to use a different colored marker to write the qualities they believe make (made) that person a great leader on the left side of the vertical line. Ask them to number each quality, which should consist of a single word or only a few words in a phrase. Tell them to list at least five, and no more than ten, leadership qualities.

   Examples might be "open-mindedness," "willingness to listen to everyone," "complimentary," "knowledge of the required results of the team," "considerate," "respectful," and so on.

   Tell participants to stay on the left side of the vertical line and to write large enough for everyone to see what they have written after their sheets are posted. (Ten minutes.)

6. Once participants have completed their lists, tell them to tape their flip-chart sheets on the wall near where they are sitting.

7. After the final sheet is posted, choose someone to present first. Ask the person to go to his or her sheet, identify the chosen model leader, and explain each of the leadership qualities that this person exhibits.

8. Permit questions (but not objections or criticisms) from the other participants and ask leading questions to help each person make a point about

leadership, if necessary. The idea is for each person to share his or her own list of desired leadership traits. (One or two minutes per participant.)

9. Refer back to the lists of leader traits throughout the workshop. Each time that a new skill has been learned, ask participants to check their lists and add what they have learned to the right side of their sheets, high-lighting that skill on the left side of their sheets if it is one possessed by their "ideal" leaders.

10. Thirty minutes prior to the close of the workshop (no matter what the work-shop's length), give each participant the opportunity to discuss the items they have written on the right side of their sheets during the course of the session. Ask them to explain any changes they have made on the left side, perhaps adding traits or deciding that the person did not really possess a particular trait. (Twenty minutes.)

11. Now ask everyone to remove the original pictures at the top of the sheets and to write their own names in place of the pictures. In other words, each of them now possesses the qualities of leadership they have previously admired in another.

12. At the close of the workshop, tell participants to remove their flip-chart sheets and take them back to their designated work areas and hang them as a reminder of the leadership skills they can now practice.

Variation

■ Ask the participants to keep in touch on a scheduled basis to see how the newly learned skills are being used by them as managers, supervisors, or team leaders.

Submitted by Richard T. Whelan.

Richard T. Whelan is the founder and director of Chesney Row Consortium for Learning & Design in Deptford, New Jersey. He writes, designs, develops, and de-livers educational learning programs designed to be used in both educational and work-related environments. The programs pertain to human resource and mental health issues or organizational issues in both the public and private sectors. His work has been published in several publications.

Introduction
to the Inventories, Questionnaires, and Surveys Section

Inventories, questionnaires, and surveys are valuable tools to the HRD professional. These feedback tools help respondents take an objective look at themselves and their organizations. These tools also help to explain how a particular theory applies to them or to their situations.

Inventories, questionnaires, and surveys are useful in a number of training and consulting situations: privately for self-diagnosis; one-on-one to plan individual development; in a small group to open discussion; in a work team to help the team to focus on its highest priorities; or in an organization to gather data to achieve progress.

You will find that the use of inventories, questionnaires, and surveys enriches, personalizes, and deepens training, development, and intervention designs. Many can be combined with other experiential learning activities or articles in this or other *Annuals* to design an exciting, involving, practical, and well-rounded intervention.

Each instrument includes the background necessary for understanding, presenting, and using it. Interpretive information, scales, and scoring sheets are also provided. In addition, we include the reliability and validity data contributed by the authors. If you wish additional information on any of these instruments, contact the authors directly. You will find their addresses and telephone numbers in the "Contributors" listing near the end of this volume.

Other assessment tools that address a wider variety of topics can be found in our comprehensive *Reference Guide to Handbooks and Annuals*. This guide indexes all the instruments that we have published to date in the *Annuals*. You will find this complete, up-to-date, and easy-to-use resource valuable for locating other instruments, as well as for locating experiential learning activities and articles.

The *2001 Annual: Volume 1, Training* includes three assessment tools in the following categories:

Individual Development

PIERS Inventory of Personal Well-Being, by Melissa I. Figueiredo, J. Elaine Kiziah, and Susan B. Wilkes

Communication

The Negotiation Continuum Questionnaire, by Nancy Jackson

Consulting and Facilitating

Change Agent Gap Analysis, by Paul L. Garavaglia

PIERS INVENTORY OF PERSONAL WELL-BEING

Melissa I. Figueiredo, J. Elaine Kiziah, and Susan B. Wilkes

Abstract: Stress and workplace wellness have become matters of increasing concern in recent years. Results from a report of a major U.S. underwriter for Workers' Compensation reveal that stress-related disorder claims increased from 6 to 13 percent from 1982 to 1990 (Northwestern National Life Insurance Company, 1991). In addition, 72 percent of the American workers sampled experienced frequent stress-related physical or mental conditions. Clearly, it could pay off to implement stress-management programs.

These programs are often designed to treat problems after they have developed. Our desire was to move from a vulnerability/deficit model of coping with stress to focus on individuals' strengths and ways of maximizing personal well-being (O'Leary & Ickovics, 1995). The concept of "thriving," the ability to grow and flourish in the face of stressors, has guided our work in developing a tool for measuring well-being. Our definition of well-being has been expanding to include emotional, spiritual, relational, and intellectual health. The PIERS Inventory of Personal Well-Being was designed to measure this multidimensional construct. It measures five dimensions of well-being relevant to an individual's sense of overall health: physical, intellectual, emotional, relational, and spiritual.

Introduction

A healthy workforce is an extremely valuable resource, but stress-related disorders are a critical threat to employee well-being. Workers' Compensation claims for psychological disorders are at record numbers, and the number of popular books about managing stress demonstrates national concern about the problem (Keita & Hurrell, 1996). Today's working Americans are facing many stressors, such as the rapid pace of change, increasing expectations for performance, and information overload. All these issues can lead to health problems. Stress in the workplace contributes to decreased productivity, increased absenteeism, and a diminished sense of personal well-being and effectiveness (Keita & Hurrell, 1996).

The concept of "thriving," the ability to grow and flourish in the face of stressors, has guided our work in developing a tool for measuring well-being (O'Leary & Ickovics, 1995). Researchers have conceptualized well-being as more than mere physical states. Attention has been directed to other aspects of well-being, such as emotional, spiritual, relational, and intellectual health. The PIERS Inventory of Personal Well-Being was designed to measure this multidimensional construct. The PIERS Inventory measures five dimensions of well-being relevant to an individual's sense of overall health: physical, intellectual, emotional, relational, and spiritual.

The use of a holistic model allows us to address the concern of some authors that there has been an artificial division between work and personal life (Frone, Russell, & Cooper, 1992; Kanter, 1977). Based on the promising role of "thriving" in enhancing employee happiness, health, and productivity, it seems worthwhile to develop interventions to increase one's ability to thrive during times of stress. As more and more organizations seek to implement stress reduction and wellness programs, new tools for measuring individual well-being are needed.

The PIERS Inventory can be used to assess participants' satisfaction with the five components of their well-being (physical, intellectual, emotional, relational, and spiritual); then consultants and trainers can develop appropriate interventions for enhancing well-being through coaching and the development of personal action plans. Practitioners who use the PIERS Inventory should possess a thorough understanding of stress management and have experience in facilitating action planning.

DESCRIPTION OF THE INSTRUMENT

The PIERS Inventory is self-scoring and contains twenty-five items, five on each of five scales deemed to be critical elements for well-being. The respondents rate the items using a seven-point Likert scale. The instrument takes from five to ten minutes to complete.

Participants can calculate their own scores. After individual scores are tabulated, participants plot their own onto flip-chart paper as part of a stress management session or workshop during which participants develop action plans for enhancing their health and improving their ability to "thrive" during times of stress.

ADMINISTRATION OF THE SURVEY

Explain that participants will take a short survey to assess their well-being. Remind them that the purpose is to gain feedback so they can learn about their levels of wellness and plan for necessary improvements in their ability to "thrive" during times of stress.

Hand out copies of the PIERS Inventory of Personal Well-Being. Instruct participants to use the full range of responses and to answer each question based on their initial reaction to each question.

EXPLANATION OF CONCEPTS

After everyone has finished, but before scoring the instrument, give a brief description of the concept of well-being and then move to an explanation of the five components used here, as described below.

Explain that stress is often recalled for its immediate physical effects on individuals, but that stress can affect us in other areas of our lives as well. Ask participants what they think of when they hear the following: physical well-being, intellectual well-being, emotional well-being, relational well-being, and spiritual well-being. After a discussion of participants' responses, hand out copies of the PIERS Definitions Sheet and read aloud the following definitions of well-being as you write them on the flip chart:

- *Physical Well-Being:* Physical well-being is comprised of a healthy body, stamina, and physical fitness.

- *Intellectual Well-Being:* Intellectual well-being refers to the ability to concentrate on mental tasks and have sharp thinking.

- *Emotional Well-Being:* Emotional well-being refers to the ability to be aware of one's feelings, as well as the ability to manage one's negative and positive emotions.

- *Relational Well-Being:* Relational well-being is a sense of connection to other people and the ability to be interdependent with others.

- *Spiritual Well-Being:* Spiritual well-being is a sense of connection to a higher power, feelings of peace, and a sense that one's life has meaning.

Tell the participants to keep these five components of well-being in mind as they interpret their scores.

SELF-SCORING INSTRUCTIONS

Hand out copies of the PIERS Self-Scoring Sheet. Tell respondents to transfer their answers and follow the instructions for calculating their scores. Assist any participants who need help.

EXPLANATION OF PIERS

Explain that the participants' overall well-being can be thought of as a "pier" on an oceanfront. Each of the five components of their well-being can be thought of as one of the "pilings" that hold up a "pier." When things are calm, the strength of the pilings is not as important. However, when a moderate to severe storm hits the "pier" (similar to when a stressful event in life occurs), the pilings must be well-developed in order to maintain the stability of the pier. By way of comparison, when we are moderately dissatisfied with our areas of well-being we can survive during times of calm, but when faced with additional stressors, we may find that our ability to "thrive" or even cope is in jeopardy.

INTERPRETATION OF THE INVENTORY

Ask everyone to examine his or her scores on their PIERS. Instruct everyone to draw their own PIERS on flip-chart paper to make a visual representation of their well-being. Demonstrate this by plotting a sample set of scores on a large piece of flip-chart paper to make a "pier" made up of five pilings labeled "PIERS." Draw a rectangle horizontally across the top of the flip-chart paper to form the top of the pier. Draw five wide rectangles vertically underneath the top of the pier and label each "piling" with one of the letters P, I, E, R, and S. Next, divide each of the five rectangles horizontally into seven segments. Fill in the seven segments, depending on the score for that scale (for example, for P = 5, you would fill in five of the seven parts for the P rectangle). Thus, each "piling" will be a different size, depending on the score for that scale. Instruct participants to be creative in designing their PIERS. For example, their strongest piling might be created with a bright color and glitter. Provide yarn, glitter, stickers, markers, chalk, paint, and other art supplies.

When participants have finished their drawings, instruct them to form groups of two or three. Hand out the PIERS Self-Reflection Worksheet and ask participants to answer the questions individually and then use their answers as a discussion guide. At the end of ten minutes, tell participants to choose one or two "pilings" or areas of well-being on which they would like to focus their efforts for repairs and/or maintenance.

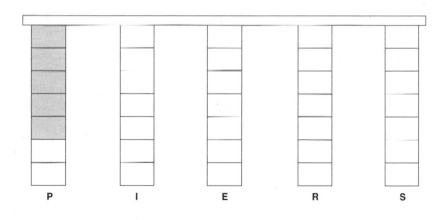

Using the Results in Action Planning

Choose one of the following activities to assist participants in creating an action plan to enhance their well-being and ability to thrive in times of stress.

1. Instruct participants to remain in their small groups. Hand out a manila envelope to each participant. Ask them to draw a tool box on the envelope or write "PIERS Tool Box" on the outside of the envelopes. (Alternatively, envelopes could be prepared beforehand with pre-drawn tool boxes on them.) Instruct participants to share their areas of repair/maintenance within their groups and ask for suggestions on how to improve or maintain these areas. Each member should write suggestions on paper and place these suggestions in the envelopes. (Paper could be precut into the shapes of different tools, or pictures of tools could be pasted to the top right-hand corner of each piece of paper.)

2. If there is not enough time for the activity above, post five pieces of flip-chart paper around the room. Label them "physical," "intellectual," "emotional," "relational," and "spiritual." Hand out five sticky notes to each person. Instruct participants to write their favorite ways to improve in each area, so that they have one idea on one sticky note for each piece of flip-chart paper. Instruct the participants to go around the room and stick their notes onto the appropriate sheets. Ask participants to then go back to their area(s) of repair/maintenance for other people's ideas and write these down to include in their "tool boxes" (manila envelopes).

Conclusion and Wrap-Up

Facilitate discussion on participants' favorite suggestions for enhancing their well-being, what they learned during the session, and the usefulness of the session for them.

Psychometric Properties of the Instrument

Demographics on the Sample

In order to test reliability of the instrument, 242 people (both university students and full-time employees from a variety of organizations) completed the PIERS Inventory. Of the employees, 22 percent were age 46 or older (40 percent were age 36 or older) and had significant work experience. Of those from whom demographic data were collected, 64.4 percent were Caucasian, 18.5 percent African-American, 8.3 percent Asian, and 8.8 percent "other." Seventy-six percent of the group was female.

Reliability

Internal consistency for the overall scale and each of the five subscales was calculated using Cronbach's alpha for the full sample of 242 participants. The internal consistency score for the overall scale of twenty-five items was very high, with an alpha of .92. Alpha coefficients for the subscales of physical, intellectual, emotional, relational, and spiritual well-being were .80, .82, .74, .81, and .80, respectively, indicating acceptable internal consistencies.

Test-retest correlations were calculated based on a sample of twenty-four individuals who took the survey once and then took it again two weeks later. The test-retest correlation for the overall survey score was .82. Test retest correlations for the subscales physical, intellectual, emotional, relational, and spiritual well-being were .83, .80, .76, .71, and .81, respectively.

References

Frone, M.R., Russell, M., & Cooper, M.L. (1992). Prevalence of work-family conflict. Are work and family boundaries asymmetrically permeable? *Journal of Organizational Behavior, 13*, 723–729.

Kanter, R.M. (1977). *Work and family in the United States.* New York: Russell Sage Foundation.

Keita, G.P., & Hurrell, J.J. (1996). *Job stress in a changing workforce.* Washington, DC: American Psychological Association.

Northwestern National Life Insurance Company. (1991). *Employee burnout: America's newest epidemic.* Minneapolis, MN: Author.

O'Leary, V.E., & Ickovics, J.R. (1995). Resilience and thriving in response to challenge: An opportunity for a paradigm shift in women's health. *Women's Health, 1*(2), 121–142.

Melissa I. Figueiredo, M.S., *is project coordinator of the Workplace Initiatives Program, a training and consulting unit in the Department of Psychology at Virginia Commonwealth University (VCU). She is a doctoral candidate in VCU's APA-accredited counseling psychology program. Her professional interests include health psychology and group dynamics. She has designed and led workshops on stress management. In addition, she has taught psychology of women and helping relations as an adjunct faculty member of VCU.*

J. Elaine Kiziah, M.S., *is program designer with the Workplace Initiatives Program, a training and consulting unit in the Department of Psychology at Virginia Commonwealth University. She is a doctoral student in VCU's APA-accredited counseling psychology program. Her professional interests focus around the intersection of positive psychology and career development/life planning. Ms. Kiziah has designed career development workshops and tools, as well as led sessions on career planning, change management, and other topics.*

Susan B. Wilkes, Ph.D., *manages the Workplace Initiatives Program, a training and consulting unit in the Department of Psychology at Virginia Commonwealth University. She is an organizational psychologist, a frequent workshop leader, consultant, and executive coach. Her areas of expertise include stress management, team performance, organizational change, performance improvement, and leadership. Dr. Wilkes is a Licensed Professional Counselor and instructor who has taught courses in psychology, stress management, group dynamics, and industrial/organizational psychology.*

PIERS Inventory of Personal Well-Being

Melissa I. Figueiredo, J. Elaine Kiziah, and Susan B. Wilkes

Instructions: Read each item below carefully. Using the scale provided, rate how satisfied you are with each aspect of your personal well-being. Select the number that best describes your response in each case and circle it.

1 = Very Dissatisfied   5 = Mildly Satisfied
2 = Dissatisfied   6 = Satisfied
3 = Mildly Dissatisfied   7 = Very Satisfied
4 = Neutral

To what extent are you satisfied with:

1. Your energy level?	1	2	3	4	5	6	7
2. Your ability to concentrate?	1	2	3	4	5	6	7
3. Your feelings of optimism about the future?	1	2	3	4	5	6	7
4. The people available for you to rely on during times of difficulty?	1	2	3	4	5	6	7
5. Your ability to find meaning in life?	1	2	3	4	5	6	7
6. The amount of physical activity you achieve?	1	2	3	4	5	6	7
7. Your ability to remember things?	1	2	3	4	5	6	7
8. Your ability to express feelings in a constructive way?	1	2	3	4	5	6	7
9. The amount of caring in your relationships?	1	2	3	4	5	6	7
10. Your peace of mind?	1	2	3	4	5	6	7
11. Your body's ability to tolerate stress?	1	2	3	4	5	6	7
12. The clarity of your thinking?	1	2	3	4	5	6	7
13. The way you keep daily hassles in perspective?	1	2	3	4	5	6	7

14. The degree of emotional intimacy in
    your relationships?   1   2   3   4   5   6   7

15. The sense of purpose in your life?   1   2   3   4   5   6   7

16. The amount and quality of sleep and
    rest you get?   1   2   3   4   5   6   7

17. The way you understand new concepts? 1   2   3   4   5   6   7

18. Your awareness of your feelings?   1   2   3   4   5   6   7

19. Your communication with other
    people?   1   2   3   4   5   6   7

20. Your connection to something larger
    than yourself?   1   2   3   4   5   6   7

21. Your eating and drinking habits?   1   2   3   4   5   6   7

22. Your problem-solving skills?   1   2   3   4   5   6   7

23. Your ability to experience life?   1   2   3   4   5   6   7

24. The degree to which you feel under-
    stood by others?   1   2   3   4   5   6   7

25. Your ability to remember what's
    really important in life?   1   2   3   4   5   6   7

PIERS DEFINITIONS SHEET

Keep the following definitions in mind as you work on improving your PIERS.

- *Physical Well-Being:* Physical well-being is comprised of a healthy body, stamina, and physical fitness.

- *Intellectual Well-Being:* Intellectual well-being refers to the ability to concentrate on mental tasks and have sharp thinking.

- *Emotional Well-Being:* Emotional well-being refers to the ability to be aware of one's feelings, as well as the ability to manage one's negative and positive emotions.

- *Relational Well-Being:* Relational well-being is a sense of connection to other people and the ability to be interdependent with others.

- *Spiritual Well-Being:* Spiritual well-being is a sense of connection to a higher power, feelings of peace, and a sense that one's life has meaning.

PIERS Self-Scoring Sheet

Instructions: Transfer your responses for each question to this page. Add up the numbers in each column to give a total score for each letter.

1. ____	2. ____	3. ____	4. ____	5. ____
6. ____	7. ____	8. ____	9. ____	10. ____
11. ____	12. ____	13. ____	14. ____	15. ____
16. ____	17. ____	18. ____	19. ____	20. ____
21. ____	22. ____	23. ____	24. ____	25. ____

Total: ____ ____ ____ ____ ____

      P   **I**   **E**   **R**   **S**

Final Score: ____ ____ ____ ____ ____
(Divide by 5) **P**   **I**   **E**   **R**   **S**

Overall Score: ____
    (Sum of Final Scores)

What does your overall score mean?

29 through 35: You are very satisfied with your well-being. Keep up the good work maintaining your PIERS.

20 through 28: You are fairly satisfied with your well-being. You could probably choose one or two of your lowest areas to "shore up."

11 through 19: You are somewhat dissatisfied with your well-being. You may be "surviving" instead of "thriving." Choose two to three areas of improvement.

5 through 10: You are very dissatisfied with your well-being. Choose two or three areas in need of repair and consider further stress management courses. Ask your facilitator for resources.

PIERS Self-Reflection Worksheet

Instructions: Answer each of the following questions in the space provided.

1. Is one of your areas weaker than the others?

2. Do all of your areas need "shoring up"?

3. Are there areas that matter most to you and are they as strong as you would like?

4. How can you maintain the pilings in your PIERS?

5. Are you satisfied with the overall picture?

6. How strong are your PIERS?

7. How might your PIERS be improved? List as many ways as possible.

THE NEGOTIATION CONTINUUM QUESTIONNAIRE

Nancy Jackson

Abstract: In the heat of a conflict, opposing parties can become so enmeshed in their positions that they become stuck. The issues become obscured in the tug of war for power and control. The Negotiation Continuum Questionnaire helps mediators and disputants make progress in negotiating the issues during such a conflict. The questionnaire and the suggested discussion can be used when parties seem stuck and unable to move forward.

INTRODUCTION

In Dave Ellis' work on student success, he uses a word-choice model to help individuals to become more powerful (Ellis & Lankowitz, 1995). The model is a seven-step ladder, that helps the individual shift the focus of thinking from feeling victimized to personal empowerment and effectiveness. On the bottom rung is *victim mud,* followed by *obligation, possibility, preference, passion, plan,* and finally *promise.* These steps represent word choices that we make that Ellis claims keep us from experiencing the power and responsibility that we truly possess. The Negotiation Continuum Questionnaire is derived from Ellis' idea that the change from feeling victimized to feeling committed can be seen as a step-by-step progression of thoughtful choices. Rather than using the ladder image, we will adopt a continuum, implying some forward and backward movement, and the nondiscrete phases of a negotiation. The concept of "victim mud" has also been changed to "stuck."

THE PROCESS

Many negotiators and mediators follow a process that helps the negotiation move toward a solution that satisfies both parties. This process may follow the common problem-solving model: (1) Define the problem, its scope and history, (2) brainstorm alternatives, (3) select the best alternative, and (4) evaluate the chosen alternative. The negotiation process can become bogged down at any of these stages. Parties may have difficulty listening to one another, may skip brainstorming and insist on a position (solution), be unable to come up with a creative alternative that suits both parties, or simply not trust one another. When the negotiation comes to a stop, disputants need to listen and clarify issues, rather than insisting on the same process that led them to a standstill in the first place. The questionnaire may be used at this point.

Using the questionnaire will help disputants clarify the process that they are using and help them, if they are committed to a solution, arrive at a common reference point for the negotiations. The questionnaire is not meant to be used as a mass assessment, but rather as a tool for those engaged in negotiation (or conflict) to take a deeper look at their particular negotiation, where it might be stuck, and then give them clues to "jump start" it back into movement. There are two ways to use the questionnaire. One way is to have both parties fill it out, compare answers, and discuss where they are and how to progress. This process may be perceived as more objective. The second way to use it is as a process guide. With this method, either party may simply refer to the questions as a measure of where the negotiation is and ask the questions as part of the negotiation process.

SAMPLE USE OF THE QUESTIONNAIRE

For example, say Stan is Glen's supervisor. Glen has burst into Stan's office, accusing Stan of being unfair for giving Annie time off, whereas Glen had to work overtime to finish a report. Glen frames the discussion as a confrontation.

> *Glen:* "I can't stand your favoritism anymore. You have really done it this time!"

Stan sees Glen as a chronic complainer. He knows that Annie has physical problems that she does not want known. Both Stan and Glen feel *stuck*. They have positions that they want to defend: "I am right and you are wrong!" This is precisely where they could look at the questionnaire and discuss options for moving forward.

In the scenario, one or both could begin by acknowledging their mutual "stuckness." Then, either with the help of a mediator or as a joint effort, they could assess their dilemma using the model. As the situation is currently framed, both are stuck in victim mud, pointing accusatory fingers at one another. To move to the second phase, they might acknowledge the *obligatory* statements they are making. Here's how the dialogue could go:

> *Ask:* What statements are you making about something that someone "should" do or something that "must" be done?
>
> *Stan:* I am the supervisor, so I must be right. I must teach Glen that he cannot tell me how to run my department! He should abide by my decisions without question!
>
> *Glen:* I must win this argument. I cannot back down just because he's my boss. He should be fair!

If both parties can only voice their statements of obligation, they can then discuss those statements and assess them for their reasonableness and accuracy. Must a supervisor always be right? Why can't Glen back down or at least try to resolve the issue? Is this a positional argument or can they reframe the issue into a problem that needs a solution? In this case, a mediator could be helpful to point out the "shoulds" and "musts." But with practice and training, anyone can learn to spot how this type of language ties the speaker to being stuck.

After Glen and Stan resolve the obligation issue, they can move to the next stage, *possibilities.* In the possibilities phase, Stan and Glen would discuss alternatives.

> *Ask:* Do you see any other possibilities that explain the other person's perspective or that could lead to a solution?
>
> *Stan:* It's possible that Glen does not understand the situation.
>
> *Glen:* It's possible that there are reasons for Stan's apparent favoritism.

Thus Glen and Stan can have a discussion about the alternative explanations and alternative solutions.

This is similar to the brainstorming phase of problem solving. Creating multiple alternatives energizes and empowers. With a variety of possibilities to explain the situation and when both parties feel that they have been heard, they can move to the *preference* phase:

> *Ask:* What solutions or aspects of a solution would you prefer? How would you like this issue to be resolved?
>
> *Stan:* I'd prefer, Glen, to work with you on solving this issue. I know that several other people in the department are concerned about lack of time off also.
>
> *Glen:* I'd prefer it if you'd level with us and involve us in your decisions. I'd like to form a committee to come up with a proposal that we could submit about overtime policy.

Once preferences are known, the movement is to *passion,* making a commitment or putting energy into a solution. The preferences can be weighed and evaluated with both parties' needs in mind. To find out what those needs and issues are, so that the best alternative can be chosen, the process moves to the next phase.

Now Stan, the supervisor, has caught on to the process and is asking the questions.

Stan: What are you primary concerns here? (that is, what is your passion?)

Glen: I just want things to be fair! I don't mind putting extra work in on this; I understand that people have personal issues that you can't share, but we do need a policy on time off.

Stan: My concerns are that the people in the department must work together and that we have reasonable policies that everyone understands. I would very much like to work with you and clear up this issue!

From passion, the movement is toward making a *plan*. Again, the supervisor takes over the process:

Stan: How can we work together to create a schedule that you would be satisfied with?

Glen: Can we form a subcommittee and make some suggestions?

A plan to work together on a mutually satisfactory solution is created. Last in the negotiation process is the *promise*.

Stan: I cannot promise that I will implement whatever you bring in, but I can promise that I will seriously consider it.

Glen: And I promise that I will get back with you by next week with some suggestions that you will like!

And thus the negotiation is completed—moving from stuck to promise. Of course, this is a fabricated scenario, but the process of using the phases and the questionnaire will guide the parties through the steps of such a negotiation when the traditional process bogs down. This continuum helps bring forth the issues and hidden agendas the parties may not even be aware of. It gives the negotiators a framework and structure that moves both through a logical process.

In the sample scenario, the parties got stuck at the beginning of their negotiation. In reality, the negotiation can get stuck at any phase. The questionnaire was designed to help disputants identify which phase they are in and take the next appropriate action. It allows the opportunity to discuss the appropriate next phase to get them moving again.

Administering the Instrument

Give disputants copies of the questionnaire. Explain the various stages of negotiation and give examples of the process from the sample negotiation above. Allow time for them to respond individually, then to share their responses and decide which stage they are in.

You can then help by facilitating the discussion, but allowing them as much freedom to move through the stages of negotiation as they are willing and able to do on their own. Keep them aware of the phase they are in so they can learn the model and use it more effectively, or even use it on their own in the future.

Reference

Ellis, D., & Lankowitz, S. (1995). *Human being: A manual for happiness, health, love and wealth.* David Ellis.

Nancy Jackson, Ph.D., is the lead coordinator (staff and faculty developer) for Red Rocks Community College and a past contributor to training activity collections. She also teaches communication, conflict, and negotiation and business courses as an adjunct faculty member. Dr. Jackson conducts workshops on communication for Nancy Jackson and Associates and has published a number of articles.

THE NEGOTIATION CONTINUUM QUESTIONNAIRE

Nancy Jackson

In a conflict situation, the disputants can become polarized and frozen in positions and may not see possibilities available to them. If you are in a negotiation, filling out the Negotiation Continuum Questionnaire below will help you to assess where you are in the power struggle and give you tools to move the negotiation.

Instructions: Mark the *pair* of statements below that is most applicable to the situation as you see it.

Stuck

_____ 1. I see no future for this conflict.

_____ 2. The other person is stubborn and I will not give in.

Obligation

_____ 3. I feel that I have to work things out, but I really don't want to.

_____ 4. The other person has to recognize my position before I will discuss the issue.

Possibility

_____ 5. There are some possibilities that we haven't explored.

_____ 6. The other person and I could brainstorm alternatives.

Preference

_____ 7. I'd prefer to have it my way, but I can see the other side's point of view.

_____ 8. The other person has something I'd rather have.

Passion

_____ 9. This is exciting; I can see a way for us both to get what we want!

_____ 10. The other person is contributing a lot of energy.

Plan

_____ 11. We can work on a plan together.

_____ 12. The other person has some ideas I'd like to use.

Promise

_____ 13. I will keep my promises and do my share.

_____ 14. The other person has made promises that will work.

Negotiation Continuum Interpretation Sheet

Instructions: Each pair of responses (1 and 2, 3 and 4, and so forth) represents one phase on a continuum from "stuck" to "promise."

Look at the continuum and the short definitions below and assess where you and the other person are as far as discussing and reaching agreement on the problem or issue.

Stuck➤ Obligation ➤ Possibility➤ Preference ➤ Passion ➤ Plan ➤ Promise

Stuck: Both parties have taken positions and are acting in an accusatory manner.

Obligation: Thoughts or statements framed as "must" or "should" that, if expressed, can help the parties see one another's positions.

Possibility: Restatements of the situation that show possible alternative ways to look at it.

Preference: Statements by each side of his or her own preferences.

Passion: Strong expression of feelings and desired results by each party—that is, what is most important to each.

Plan: Working together on a mutually satisfactory solution that takes each person's passion into account.

Promise: A commitment to act on the plan on the part of each person.

Now look at your results and answer the questions below so that together you can find a way to move to the next stage of the continuum.

Do you both agree on the stage your negotiation is in? This is a good starting point. (A fruitful discussion can still take place if you and the other person disagree about where you are at this point.)

Make some notes for a discussion of trust, your history of past negotiations, or other issues. (This may clarify hidden agendas or other issues one or both of you may have bearing on the conflict.)

What unresolved issues do you have between you that you could discuss at this point?

Look at where you are now on the continuum and see whether you can take a next step. For example, can you see a possibility or state a preference?

1. For example, if you decide that your discussion is stuck in the first phase, consider moving to the second phase, obligation, by considering the reasons why you should or ought to negotiate the conflict. What is dependant on the outcome? What are possible losses?

2. To move from obligation to possibility, brainstorm alternatives and possibilities. What would the situation look like if it were solved? What resources can be put into play?

3. To move from possibility to preference, brainstorm some possibilities and discuss the alternatives and your preferred solutions. Avoid taking the position of "I must have this," but rather try discussing your preferences with statements such as, "I'd like to have this because. . . ."

4. You can try to move from preference to passion by discussing your preferred solutions. By discussing both of your preferred solutions, the energy from both points of view is combined and you can work toward a common goal more easily.

5. The move from passion (your major concern) to making a plan for action seems almost automatic. Now you can decide who does what, the time lines, any concessions, and how to distribute resources.

6. Last is the move from plan of action to promise to fulfill the plan. It involves a commitment from both of you to carry out your portion of the plan. In a formal mediation session, the agreement or promise would be written and signed.

As you and the other person move through the various phases, you will have completed a process of problem solving. You can use the steps outlined above and the questionnaire every time you're in a similar situation, either on your own or in a facilitated session, to reach a thoughtful, issue-focused, empowering solution.

CHANGE AGENT GAP ANALYSIS

Paul L. Garavaglia

Abstract: Is CHANGE an acronym for Can't Handle Another Nonproductive Grandiose Escapade? Or will embracing change and adapting effectively to the demands it brings go a long way toward the improvement of business processes and organizational and personal effectiveness? It has been suggested that using a change management framework to help make training "stick" makes good sense. After all, the point of most training is transfer of learning or behavioral change. Applying what is learned in training back on the job can help increase both individual and organizational performance. Therefore, it is important for change agents to assess their own ability to assist an organization during a change effort.

INTRODUCTION

Businesses often fail to realize the level of effort, work, dedication, and leadership required to respond to change successfully. Instead we give creative titles—re-engineering, business process improvement, transformation, realignment, organization development initiative, and so forth—to the type of activities that come under the change management umbrella, juggle some resources and activities for awhile, and wonder why the majority of change management efforts fail. Unfortunately, change management is not a neat sequential process, and organizations often automatically adopt new technologies and new approaches to management without determining how well they fit their business strategy, whether they are in fact needed, or whether they have the organizational capabilities to implement the change. For change to be effective and continuous, a process has to be put in place that balances learning new practices with maintaining stability in key capabilities.

Learning to embrace change and adapt effectively to the demands it brings will go a long way toward the improvement of business processes, as well as toward organizational and personal effectiveness. Additionally, learning and development should be taken seriously. We, as change agents, have to take time to plan change, manage it, and evaluate it if we are going to exist in a rapidly changing competitive environment. Understanding that training is not just a one-time event, but a process that over time needs to be reviewed, analyzed, enhanced, updated, refined, changed, and improved, allows us to understand how change management and training are linked.

DESCRIPTION OF THE ASSESSMENT

This assessment for change agents addresses the following four areas, which often create problems in a change environment:

- Envisioning
- Communicating
- Training
- Organizing

Ten change management related transfer action items that may come prior to, during, or succeeding a training event are assessed for each area. For example, the ability to envision is broken into five actions to be done prior to training, one action to take after training, and four actions to take following training. Communicating has four actions to be done preceding training, one during training, and five after training. Training has five actions to be done preceding training, three during training, and two after training. Organizing has six actions to be done preceding training, two during training, and two after training. Use the following chart as a reference.

Change Management Related Transfer Actions			
A. Envisioning—"see it"	Preceding	During	Afterward
Approve use of confidential organizational data as resources for training.	✔		
Require attendance at training for certain categories of employees.	✔		
Select trainees according to established criteria for that training program.	✔		
Select trainees on basis of training plans for each employee.	✔		
Authorize more time for trainee to perform tasks, applying new behaviors for a short period after returning to the job.	✔		
Arrange for organization to use products developed by trainees.		✔	
Set mutual expectations for improvement.			✔
Practice ways to reinforce use of new job behaviors by trainee.			✔
Help trainee set realistic goals for job performance.			✔
Assign trainee to supervisor who is a good role model and encourages use of new skills.			✔

Change Management Related Transfer Actions			
B. Communicating—"tell it and sell it"	**Preceding**	**During**	**Afterward**
Participate in advance briefing of managers and supervisors about training program.	✔		
Brief trainee on course objectives, content, process, and application to the job.	✔		
Confer with employee on reasons for selection for training.	✔		
Confer with employee on performance expectations following training.	✔		
Communicate support for the program.		✔	
Involve trainee in work-related decisions based on new learning.			✔
Have regular individual conferences with trainee back on the job.			✔
Inform trainee of regularly increased expectations for levels of performance.			✔
Regularly report data on trainees' use of new behaviors.			✔
Publicize successes.			✔
C. Training—"teach it"	**Preceding**	**During**	**Afterward**
Participate in preview of training program.	✔		
Provide supervisory coaching skills.	✔		
Participate in one or more training sessions attended by employees.	✔		
Allow trainee preparation time before training sessions.	✔		
Assist trainee, as requested, with required assignments.	✔		

Change Management Related Transfer Actions			
C. Training—"teach it" *(continued)*	Preceding	During	Afterward
Authorize alternate cycles of training, practical application on the job, and return to training.		✔	
Release trainee from normal duties during training.		✔	
Participate in transfer action planning.		✔	
Arrange later follow-up workshop for trainee reports on projects and action plans.			✔
Provide occasional practice sessions for important but seldom-used skills.			✔
D. Organizing—"define it"	Preceding	During	Afterward
Actively participate in assessment of training needs.	✔		
Actively participate in design of training program.	✔		
Collect baseline performance data.	✔		
Build transfer of training into supervisory performance standards.	✔		
Contribute to development of criteria for selecting employees for training.	✔		
Develop a supervisor/trainee contract.	✔		
Study data on new trainees about to arrive on the job after training.		✔	
Plan assessment of transfer of new skills to the job.		✔	
Develop opportunities for trainee to use new behaviors immediately on the job.			✔
Provide behavioral checklists to trainees as self-feedback instruments.			✔

The respondent (change agent) rates each change management related transfer action in terms of his or her *current* level of performance and his or her *potential* level of performance. This tells the respondent the "as is," "existing," or "current" state, as well as the "to be," "desired," or "future" state. Comparing the two states allows respondents to discover gaps in their performance quickly and easily. The change agent can then analyze the gap between his or her current and potential levels of performance to determine practices needed to make training stick.

ADMINISTRATION OF THE ASSESSMENT

The assessment is meant to be used for self-improvement. Typically, supervisors and managers take the instrument in order to assess their ability to function as change agents before, during, and after a change effort. It is advised that the results be assessed with an HRD professional in a training setting. Following are some general guidelines for using the assessment:

1. The assessment can be completed individually, in work groups, or as part of a larger meeting. It can be administered company-wide or stratified to represent each individual department or work group in an organization.

2. This is a simple, easy-to-complete, yet profoundly powerful assessment, so sample as many supervisors and managers within an organization as possible.

3. Provide a brief explanation of the purpose of the assessment. Build commitment by explaining the goals and benefits of the assessment (to identify current and potential levels for performing change management related transfer actions) in the organization at this time.

4. Inform respondents that they will be asked to circle the answer that best represents their own behavior and that after they are finished you will provide an explanation.

5. End the assessment with the appropriate closing discussion. The total time taken to complete the assessment itself ranges from twenty to thirty minutes, with about the same amount of time or more needed for scoring and discussion afterward.

Alternatively, you can use the assessment results in a group to form individual action plans that identify how to go from one's current level of ability to a desired level of ability. A good action plan would consist of goals and objectives, as well as a time commitment, a discussion of barriers that might hinder performance, solutions to those problems, resources needed, and the steps and actions to take, a budget for projected costs, and a listing of benefits to be obtained.

PRESENTATION OF THE THEORY

The best way to present the theory behind the assessment is to explain that change efforts provide an opportunity for training managers in the many ways to affect key business practices. If in fact we are sending people to training to learn new behaviors or to change old behaviors, it is imperative that we implement a training process that balances learning new practices with maintaining stability. In fact, envisioning the desired future is an excellent approach to any change effort—and certainly to making the individual changes needed before a change effort can be successful. One way to make sure that training is successful is to discover the ways we now use to "tell it and sell it" so that we can learn better ways to convince others of the need to change so that the change can become ingrained into our daily operations. The same is true for how we "teach" the new ways, not as much from an instructional design and delivery perspective, but from an organization development perspective, looking at the organizational climate, work group support, and pace of the workflow. Finally, when organizing we "define" what we expect and structure our training initiatives to optimize the chances for success. For each of the four classifications within the change management framework, managers can be taught to help others transfer learning into action. The key is to train managers and supervisors in ways that help them to change their own behavior prior to rolling out a change event within an organization.

Unfortunately, many organizations are not set up to support trainees back on the job because they do not see individual change as the goal. They assume that the trainees will apply what was learned on their own. We can make training and change efforts more effective by making them more comprehensive. Training must be undertaken to meet specific needs of the organization. Training will be more easily incorporated organization-wide if the change agents are reinforced on the job as they train others.

Scoring the Assessment

All items on the assessment receive a rating between 0 and 5. Zero represents a change management related transfer action that is *never* or rarely engaged in, whereas 5 represents a change management related transfer action that is *always* engaged in. Each respondent circles the answer that best describes his or her own behavior for each of the forty actions. When respondents are finished, have them add the numbers they have circled in each column to obtain their totals for both *current* and *potential* levels for each of the categories. Next, have them determine the gap between their current and potential levels.

Interpreting the Scores

A total score of 50 is possible for both current and potential levels. Theoretically, the gap for each category could be as high as 50, but this is not likely. If the gap between current and potential is small, not as much work is needed. However, if the gap is large, the respondent needs work to improve in this area. The following scale should be used to interpret scores for each of the four areas:

Gap Between Scores	Description
More than 35 points	You need to improve before attempting to help others through a change effort.
29 to 35 points	You have the idea, but need to improve before you can be useful to others.
22 to 28 points	You have the potential to become a change agent.
15 to 21 points	You are almost a change agent.
Fewer than 15 points	You are a change agent. Keep up the good work.

Posting the Scores

Cumulative change management related transfer action scores for each category (envisioning, communicating, training, and organizing), as well as a cumulative score obtained by totaling each of the four categories, should be shared among participants in small discussion groups, which will help to facilitate learning. Subgroups can each come up with action items for turning low change management related scores into high scores. Once specific action items are determined, the respondents must be accountable for making the necessary changes. Group members can agree to follow up with one another to be sure changes are made.

RELIABILITY AND VALIDITY

Over one hundred assessments were completed by volunteers and the assessment was determined to be reliable in test re-test studies. Over one hundred fifty transfer and change management references were reviewed to come up with the forty change management related actions that form the assessment. There was consistency within the literature, but this provides only face validity.

Paul L. Garavaglia is a principal consultant for The ADDIE Group, Inc. He is the author of the book Transfer of Training: Making Training Stick. *He is also a two-time winner of the American Society for Training and Development's Instructional Technology Blue Ribbon Award, once for the job aid "Making the Transfer Process Work" and also for the handbook "Managers As Transfer Agents." Mr. Garavaglia has published transfer-related articles in* Corporate University Review, Educational Technology, Performance Improvement, *and* Training & Development.

GAP ANALYSIS FOR CHANGE AGENTS

Paul L. Garavaglia

Instructions: Consider your role as a change agent. Read carefully each of the following change management related transfer actions that are under your control. Assess each action on a scale of 0 to 5 (0 = rarely engage in; 5 = always engage in).

In Column 1, assess your *current* level of how often you perform each action by circling the appropriate number. Answer honestly about how often you actually perform each action in your work.

In Column 2, assess your *potential* to perform each action by circling the appropriate number. Remember to answer within the limits of your own ability or ability you would like to possess, respectively.

When Envisioning, I . . .	Current Level	Potential Level
Approve use of confidential organizational data as resources for training.	0 1 2 3 4 5	0 1 2 3 4 5
Require attendance at training for certain categories of employees.	0 1 2 3 4 5	0 1 2 3 4 5
Select trainees according to established criteria for that training program.	0 1 2 3 4 5	0 1 2 3 4 5
Select trainees on the basis of training plans for each employee.	0 1 2 3 4 5	0 1 2 3 4 5
Authorize more time for trainees to perform tasks, applying new behaviors for a short period after returning to the job.	0 1 2 3 4 5	0 1 2 3 4 5
Arrange for the organization to use products developed by trainees.	0 1 2 3 4 5	0 1 2 3 4 5
Set mutual expectations for improvement.	0 1 2 3 4 5	0 1 2 3 4 5
Practice ways to reinforce use of new job behaviors by trainees.	0 1 2 3 4 5	0 1 2 3 4 5

When Envisioning, I . . .   **Current Level**   **Potential Level**

Help trainees set realistic goals for
job performance.   0 1 2 3 4 5   0 1 2 3 4 5

Assign trainees to a supervisor who is
a good role model and encourages
use of new skills.   0 1 2 3 4 5   0 1 2 3 4 5

Envisioning Totals: _____   _____

When Communicating, I . . .   **Current Level**   **Potential Level**

Participate in advance briefing of
managers and supervisors on train-
ing programs.   0 1 2 3 4 5   0 1 2 3 4 5

Brief trainees on course objectives,
content, process, and application
to the job.   0 1 2 3 4 5   0 1 2 3 4 5

Confer with employees on reasons
for selecting the training.   0 1 2 3 4 5   0 1 2 3 4 5

Confer with employees on performance expectations following
training.   0 1 2 3 4 5   0 1 2 3 4 5

Communicate support for the
program.   0 1 2 3 4 5   0 1 2 3 4 5

Involve trainees in work-related
decisions based on new learning.   0 1 2 3 4 5   0 1 2 3 4 5

Have regular individual confer-
ences with trainees back on the job. 0 1 2 3 4 5   0 1 2 3 4 5

Inform trainees of regularly
increased expectations for levels
of performance.   0 1 2 3 4 5   0 1 2 3 4 5

Regularly report data on trainees'
use of new behaviors.   0 1 2 3 4 5   0 1 2 3 4 5

Publicize successes.   0 1 2 3 4 5   0 1 2 3 4 5

Communicating Totals: _____   _____

When Training, I . . .	Current Level	Potential Level
Participate in preview of training programs.	0 1 2 3 4 5	0 1 2 3 4 5
Provide supervisory coaching skills.	0 1 2 3 4 5	0 1 2 3 4 5
Participate in one or more training sessions attended by employees.	0 1 2 3 4 5	0 1 2 3 4 5
Allow trainees preparation time before training sessions.	0 1 2 3 4 5	0 1 2 3 4 5
Assist trainees, as requested, with required assignments.	0 1 2 3 4 5	0 1 2 3 4 5
Authorize alternate cycles of training, practical application on the job, and return to training.	0 1 2 3 4 5	0 1 2 3 4 5
Release trainees from normal duties during training.	0 1 2 3 4 5	0 1 2 3 4 5
Participate in transfer action planning.	0 1 2 3 4 5	0 1 2 3 4 5
Arrange later follow-up workshop for trainee reports on projects and action plans.	0 1 2 3 4 5	0 1 2 3 4 5
Provide occasional practice sessions for important but seldom-used skills.	0 1 2 3 4 5	0 1 2 3 4 5

Training Totals: _____ _____

When Organizing, I . . .	Current Level	Potential Level
Actively participate in assessment of training needs.	0 1 2 3 4 5	0 1 2 3 4 5
Actively participate in design of training program.	0 1 2 3 4 5	0 1 2 3 4 5
Collect baseline performance data.	0 1 2 3 4 5	0 1 2 3 4 5
Build transfer of training into supervisory performance standards.	0 1 2 3 4 5	0 1 2 3 4 5

When Organizing, I . . .	Current Level	Potential Level
Contribute to development of criteria for selecting employees for training.	0 1 2 3 4 5	0 1 2 3 4 5
Develop a supervisor/trainee contract.	0 1 2 3 4 5	0 1 2 3 4 5
Study data on new trainees about to arrive on the job after training.	0 1 2 3 4 5	0 1 2 3 4 5
Plan assessment of transfer of new skills to the job.	0 1 2 3 4 5	0 1 2 3 4 5
Develop opportunities for trainees to use new behaviors immediately on the job.	0 1 2 3 4 5	0 1 2 3 4 5
Provide behavioral checklists to trainees as self-feedback instruments.	0 1 2 3 4 5	0 1 2 3 4 5

Organizing Totals: _____ _____

After you have responded to all of the items and totaled your current and *potential* levels for each area, copy your potential totals to the grid below and sum the numbers.

Envisioning	+ Communi-cating	+ Training	+ Organizing	= Total Potential Level

Copy your *current* level scores to the grid below and sum the numbers.

Envisioning	+ Communi-cating	+ Training	+ Organizing	= Total Potential Level

To determine your gap, subtract your total current level from your total potential level.

Total Potential – Total Current = _____
                                    Gap

Gap Analysis

Gap	Description
More than 35 points	You need to improve before attempting to help others through a change effort.
29 to 35 points	You have the idea, but still need to improve before you can be useful to others.
22 to 28 points	You have the potential to become a change agent.
15 to 21 points	You are almost a change agent.
Fewer than 15 points	You are a change agent. Keep up the good work.

Introduction
to the Presentation and Discussion Resources Section

The Presentation and Discussion Resources Section is a collection of articles of use to every facilitator. The theories, background information, models, and methods will challenge facilitators' thinking, enrich their professional development, and assist their internal and external clients with productive change. These articles may be used as a basis for lecturettes, as handouts in training sessions, or as background reading material.

This section will provide you with a variety of useful ideas, theoretical opinions, teachable models, practical strategies, and proven intervention methods. The articles will add richness and depth to your training and consulting knowledge and skills. They will challenge you to think differently, explore new concepts, and experiment with new interventions. The articles will continue to add a fresh perspective to your work.

The 2001 Annual: Volume 1, Training includes nine articles, in the following categories:

Individual Development: Developing Awareness and Understanding

Preventing Sexual Harassment: Stop Shortchanging Your Organization with Diversion Programs, by Harriet Cohen and Debbie Newman

Individual Development: Personal Growth

Knowledge Is Not Power; Creativity Is!, by Marlene Caroselli

Communication: Technology

The Toolmaking Business: A New Arena for Performance Technologists, by Shonn R. Colbrunn, Michelina (Micki) Juip, and Darlene M. Van Tiem

Leading E-Learning, by Brooke Broadbent

Consulting: Consulting Strategies and Techniques

How to Increase Training Effectiveness with Systems Thinking, by Gary Schouborg

Facilitating: Theories and Models of Facilitating

How to Be a World-Class Facilitator of Learning,
by Robert C. Preziosi and Kitty Preziosi

Facilitating: Techniques and Strategies

Creatively Debriefing Group Activities, by Andy Beaulieu

Customized Problem-Solving and Decision-Making Activities,
by Donald T. Simpson

Leadership: Top-Management Issues and Concerns

Creating Relationship and Agreement: "You Get What You Ask For,"
by Neil J. Simon

As with previous *Annuals,* this volume covers a wide variety of topics. The range of articles presented encourages thought-provoking discussion about the present and future of HRD. Other articles on specific subjects can be located by using our comprehensive *Reference Guide to Handbooks and Annuals.* The guide is updated regularly and indexes the contents of all the *Annuals* and the *Handbooks of Structured Experiences.* With each revision, the *Reference Guide* becomes a complete, up-to-date, and easy-to-use resource for selecting appropriate materials from the *Annuals* and *Handbooks.*

Here and in the *Reference Guide,* we have done our best to categorize the articles for easy reference; however, many of the articles encompass a range of topics, disciplines, and applications. If you do not find what you are looking for under one category, check a related category. In some cases we may place an article in the "Training" *Annual* that also has implications for "Consulting," and vice versa. As the field of HRD continues to grow and develop, there is more and more crossover between training and consulting. Explore all the contents of both volumes of the *Annual* in order to realize the full potential for learning and development that each offers.

Preventing Sexual Harassment: Stop Shortchanging Your Organization with Diversion Programs

Harriet Cohen and Debbie Newman

Abstract: Hostile work environments hold far-reaching consequences for organizations and employees, but the financial impact of court awards, case settlements, and litigation expenses pales in comparison to the effect of a demoralized workforce. Reduced productivity, increased absenteeism, surging employee turnover, compromised public image, and operational ineffectiveness are among the consequences in store for organizations that fail to transcend sexual harassment compliance programs and address the real challenges that sabotage employee achievement and organizational success.

This article is intended to persuade the reader to abandon sexual harassment diversion programs (programs targeted at perceived "at risk" populations) in favor of experiential programs that create greater understanding of ourselves and others and inspire participants to collaborate to create tangible and specific action plans to co-create more positive work environments.

INTRODUCTION

You are shortchanging your organization with traditional sexual harassment prevention and diversion programs that emphasize the magnitude of litigation awards to scare participants into compliance and that feature examples of offensive behaviors to be avoided. Although such programs may help organizations comply with legal prescriptions to minimize liability, they paradoxically lead to an increase in harassment complaints, aggravate the very behaviors they seek to extinguish, and further alienate men and women, homosexuals and heterosexuals, and employers and employees (Hammond, 1996).

It is not surprising that organizations and employees are resistant to traditional sexual harassment prevention programs. Who can blame them? Who among us wants to spend a day, a half-day, or even an hour in a program that resembles a disciplinary trip to the principal's office? Who is motivated to attend a program that seeks to turn co-workers into detectives and witnesses? Why would anyone want to participate in a diversion program?

Unfortunately, most sexual harassment prevention programs are, in essence, "singing to the choir." Most employees are not sexual predators. Most employees are not harassing co-workers. Most employees believe they behave appropriately—and even honorably—in the workplace.

So if these traditional sexual harassment prevention programs don't work, why do so many organizations invest valuable time and money in them? One reason is that organizations are afraid of complaints about a hostile work environment. These organizations have been convinced that they will reduce their legal exposure to harassment charges if they:

- Adopt a "no sexual harassment" policy;
- Vigorously communicate that policy;
- Document enforcement procedures;
- Aggressively respond to complaints; and
- Enforce their stated no-harassment policies.

Whether or not these efforts satisfy legal requirements or minimize financial exposure is debatable. What is known is that these efforts do little to prepare employees to deal effectively with interpersonal collisions that are inevitable when two or more individuals interact. When an organization limits its focus to compliance, it misses a golden opportunity to leverage organizational and individual effectiveness by setting a tone of appreciation, respect, and tolerance.

WHY TRADITIONAL PROGRAMS DON'T WORK

There are many reasons why traditional diversion and prevention programs fail to work. Most undermine their own objectives in one or more ways.

Focusing on "Behaviors to Avoid" Paradoxically Produces the Undesirable Behavior. Don't think of pink elephants in yellow leotards dancing on the rim of a champagne glass. (You are thinking about those pink elephants, right?) Don't touch the wet paint. (You are compelled to touch the paint to see whether it really is wet, right?) Don't tell anyone about the pending downsizing. (You are thinking about whom you can trust with the secret, right?)

Traditional sexual harassment prevention programs are full of "don'ts." Don't touch. Don't tell jokes. Don't flirt. Don't comment on someone's appearance. Don't use bad language. Don't post pictures. Although these "don'ts" may constitute good guidelines, the first action a participant is likely to take after spending a day inundated with "don'ts" is to "do."

Presenting "Us-Against-Them" Scenarios Amplifies Hostility in the Workplace. Polarizing men and women, heterosexuals and homosexuals, employers and employees, and victims and victimizers results in the erosion of employee morale and compromises any hope of improving interpersonal relationships in the workplace. "He said, she said" examples actually lead participants to become defensive, guarded, and understandably suspicious of one another. "He's the victimizer and she's the victim." "She seduced him and he's being set up." No matter how these collisions are characterized, the schisms are often left unresolved and participants are no more prepared to deal with tension between genders after the program concludes than they were at the outset.

It is natural for individuals to take sides in conflicts. When we successfully persuade participants to label behaviors as "good" or "bad" and then provide examples portraying one gender as victim and the other as victimizer, it is only natural for individuals to "do the math" and characterize one gender as good and the other bad. Either/or thinking does little to inspire individuals to share accountability and responsibility to work toward co-creating a hostility-free environment.

Fear-Based Programs Designed to Frighten Organizations and Participants into Compliance Do Not Work.   The cost of litigation pales in comparison to the expense associated with decreased employee morale, increased workplace hostility, and loss of trust among employees and between employees and employers. Organizations stunned by the magnitude of high-profile jury verdicts are equally surprised to learn that plaintiffs prove only a fraction of their allegations and that appeals courts overturn or significantly reduce many of the multi-million-dollar jury awards of lower courts (Risser, 1999).

The real cost to an organization stems from the lure of workplace gossip and its impact on employee morale. The direct payroll cost alone of hours spent in grapevine chatter can be staggering, particularly when compounded by the cost of escalating absenteeism, increased workplace accidents due to inattention, compromises in productivity, lost opportunity/business, destroyed reputations, and the difficulty of retaining staff.

It is not surprising that participants who are required to attend compliance-based diversion programs become suspicious and critical of the motives of the sponsoring organization. Participants are understandably cynical about programs in which concerns about fiscal liability overshadow a genuine concern about individuals and promoting respect in the workplace.

Resistant Participants Do Not Abandon Familiar Behaviors.   The old adages "you can attract more flies with honey than with vinegar" and "you can lead a horse to water but can't make it drink" apply here. Normal people become understandably defensive when they feel attacked, threatened, accused, or criticized. So-called sexual harassment prevention programs that criticize participant behavior, malign intentions, or attempt to frighten attendees into obedience with threats of personal liability and termination may attract participant attention, but also activate participant defenses and resistance.

It is illogical to think that traditional compliance or diversion programs will cure pathological perpetrators of abusive behavior. Serial victimizers will not suddenly "see the light" and spontaneously reform. Participants who are unaware of their role in creating a hostile work environment are not likely to realize suddenly that they are enablers by listening to a recitation of legal and organizational policies and procedures or by watching a few videotapes.

Most people *intend* to behave appropriately and believe they are not part of the problem. Consequently, participants will fiercely resist a program that suggests they may be directly or indirectly enabling an environment of hostility and disrespect. In the alternative, participants may become so reactive to the potential consequences of breaking the rules or crossing the line that they will lose confidence, feel threatened, and disengage from their colleagues, rendering moot any hope of building cooperative teams and optimizing organizational success.

It is neither necessary nor effective to subject participants to programming that is threatening, coercive, or fear-based. Participants yearn for respect and appreciation and will embrace programming that celebrates past and present successes and uses these "rights" as a springboard to future successes.

Program Leaders Must Be Expert Facilitators Who Have Worked Through Their Personal Biases.   Otherwise, programs will fail and participants will not be served. If an environment of respect and tolerance is to endure, participants must acquire the skills to interpret organizational policies, behave within organizational and personal boundaries, and resolve conflicts that will undoubtedly occur. If participants are to trust themselves and one another to succeed in the workplace, they must have the opportunity to experiment with and practice new behaviors within the safety and structure of a carefully designed learning environment in which they feel respected and supported.

Any program that encourages participants to explore and share personal values and opinions is likely to evoke impassioned discussion. Participants who are learning communication skills will undoubtedly make statements that are not only politically incorrect, but which may incite intense reactions from their peers. Program facilitators must be able to manage these escalating exchanges without taking sides, without imposing personal judgments, without undermining the participants' ability to save face, and without thwarting continued learning.

This process of learning should not be compromised or contaminated by the values of the program leader. Program neutrality can be achieved if the program leader is an accomplished facilitator who has engaged in a process of self-discovery that has produced an awareness of personal bias and an ability and willingness to keep these biases out of the learning experience. One way to maintain gender balance during the learning experience is to offer programs co-facilitated by male/female teams. Another way is to assess the program facilitator's ability to remain affirming and impartial.

Program Content

Programming to prevent sexual harassment and to create hostility-free work environments fails the sponsoring organization when dissemination of factual information subordinates or eclipses a focus on interpersonal skill building. However, some factual information must be presented. At the conclusion of any diversion program, participants should be able to:

- Define sexual harassment and recognize inappropriate behaviors;
- State the organization's policy on sexual harassment; and
- Detail procedures for reporting and handling harassment complaints.

Although these outcomes may contribute to creating a baseline awareness of the topic, they will not lead to an appreciable change in behavior. Leveraging employee achievement and organizational success requires programming that:

- Builds trust and enhanced team spirit;
- Celebrates individual achievement, appreciates differences, and respects uniqueness;
- Improves employee confidence and competence in interpersonal communications;
- Increases employees' sense of individual value to the organization; and
- Mobilizes employees to share accountability and responsibility to work toward co-creating a hostility-free work environment.

In most cases, charges of hostility are the consequence of good intentions gone awry. Misinterpreted behaviors and interpersonal communication skills that are inadequate to correct these misunderstandings make an organization susceptible to reduced productivity, increased absenteeism, employee retention challenges, compromised public image, operational ineffectiveness, increased complaints, litigation, and retaliation. Organizations that have assessed the magnitude of these consequences in tangible and intangible terms would insist on sexual harassment prevention programming that is focused on helping participants:

- Become aware of and learn to communicate personally held values, beliefs, attitudes, feelings, and behaviors;

- Discover and respect the values, beliefs, attitudes, feelings, and behaviors of others;

- Recognize and take responsibility for the impact of one's own behaviors on others; and

- Develop action plans to modify, amplify, or extinguish behaviors that enable hostile work environments.

INTERVENTION STRATEGIES

When designing or evaluating a sexual harassment prevention program, or any program for that matter, the analyst should carefully consider the underlying theories on which the program is based. Most diversion programs are based on the assumption that it is more likely than not that participants cannot or will not avoid the temptation to engage in insulting, inappropriate, abusive, and antisocial behaviors. Although these assumptions might be accurate for a population of perpetrators and individuals who have already exhibited behaviors that suggest they are likely to perpetrate, it is inaccurate to apply these assumptions to the general population. The majority of our audiences do not act with malice. They are well-meaning people whose intentions are honorable. What an insult to deliver a program that is based on an assumption that all participants are the same as the few who have no conscience and no self-control.

Systems thinking, polarity management, appreciative inquiry, and dialogue interventions are among underlying theories that should be driving the design and development of sexual harassment prevention programming for the general population.

Systems Thinking

Mahatma Gandhi suggested that "we should become the change we seek in the world." An environment of tolerance and respect can start with one individual and grow as others who are similarly predisposed join together to form communities of tolerance and respect.

Participants in harassment prevention programs will be more inclined to embrace workplace values that align with their personal beliefs, attitudes, and feelings. We begin by inviting participants to look inward to inventory personal views about their own gender, about the other gender, and about sexual orientations. Individuals then get together with others of their own gender to identify shared and divergent values, beliefs, and feelings. After each gender group has clarified its own shared values, the whole group is reunited to discover the values, beliefs, feelings, and experiences the members share and those that are not shared. It is at this point that the whole group can begin to initiate tangible and specific action plans for moving forward together.

Polarity Management

Key to any healthy relationship, in or out of the workplace, is achieving a dynamic balance that values each party and attends to the respective needs of all individuals who work together. This is not a situation for either/or thinking. All employees must be valued and no one can be sacrificed in the service of another if workplace relationships are to remain healthy and mutually affirming. Meeting the needs of all parties, simultaneously and consistently, is crucial to the success of the individual, the team, and the organization; but attending to everyone's individual and collective needs is difficult and problematic. Over time, maintaining the delicate balance among the opposing priorities of individuals is a challenge riddled with tension and conflict. Expectations to achieve tension-free interactions in hostility-free work environments are unrealistic and misguided. Although we can aspire to achieve this ideal, we must be realistic and recognize that there is no such thing as a tension-free or hostility-free work environment.

The application of *polarity management* theory will help participants set expectations for themselves and others that are more realistic and achievable. This is particularly important when organizations establish outcome expectations for sexual harassment prevention programs. Tension between genders is inevitable and necessary. The goal is not to eliminate this tension, but to manage it effectively so that both men and women feel valued, respected, and supported in the workplace.

Appreciative Inquiry Theory

Participants are more likely to embrace change when they can build on familiar behaviors already mastered. A complete behavioral makeover is rarely necessary. Future success is possible when action is launched from a foundation of what already works. Success is more likely when participants are confident in their ability to do well. A program that uses the language of honor and respect will generate honor and respect. Focusing on hostility creates hostility. Focusing on tolerance creates tolerance. Practicing a philosophy of appreciation will go a long way to produce an environment that embraces respect and appreciation as core values.

Dialogue Techniques

Communication is the key to creating the trust necessary for exorcising intolerance and hostility from the workplace. Dialogue is a technique that can enable participants to expand their focus from the work they do to how they do the work. Experience with and in dialogue can equip participants with the skills and ability to express themselves more fully, to listen without interrupting, to inquire and reflect without distorting a message with personal judgments and assumptions, and to value both verbal and nonverbal forms of expression. The dialogue process can help participants build relationships with one another that can move them toward a more affirming workplace environment.

CONCLUSION

So-called sexual harassment prevention programs that fail to emphasize interpersonal skill building lure sponsoring organizations into a false sense of security and paradoxically undermine or aggravate the very behaviors and relationships they seek to improve. An interpersonal skills program with the potential to provide a substantial return on the investment of time and funds will:

- Showcase and promote acceptable behaviors already exhibited in the workplace;
- Help participants find their own voices to speak for themselves, and only themselves, when communicating concerns;
- Model appropriate ways to express appreciation, interest, approval, and disapproval of workplace behaviors;
- Create opportunities for participants to practice the skills necessary to manage interpersonal tension and resolve interpersonal conflict;
- Help participants set realistic expectations for themselves and others;
- Improve participants' perception of self-worth and self-confidence; and
- Celebrate diversity, tolerance, and respect.

References

Ellinor, L., & Gerard, G. (1998). *Dialogue: Rediscover the transforming power of conversation.* New York: John Wiley.

Hammond, S. (1996). *The thin book of appreciative inquiry.* Plano, TX: Thin Book Publishing.

Johnson, B. (1992). *Polarity management: Identifying and managing unsolvable problems.* Amherst, MA: HRD Press.

Kipnis, A., & Herron, E. (1995). *What women & men really want.* Novato, CA: Nataraj Publishing.

Risser, R. (1999, August). Sexual harassment training: Truth and consequences. *Training & Development.*

Harriet Cohen, *president of Training Solutions, provides expert external resources to improve performance. She has twenty years' experience in team dynamics, performance management, strategic planning, marketing, and customer driven quality. Ms. Cohen has first-hand knowledge of business strategies and procedures that, combined with training skills, offer both practical and theoretical information to excel in today's marketplace. A leader in ASTD, she was the 1995 ASTD-LA president and West Coast field consultant for national ASTD.*

Debbie Newman *is a respected facilitator and diagnostician, specializing in the identification and resolution of work-related conflict, stress, and demoralization. She established a performance consulting and counseling practice, Working Relationships, to help individual and institutional clients leverage employee and organizational success in an atmosphere that embraces diversity and promotes respect for the individual. She is accomplished in the practice of performance consulting, relationship counseling, instructional design, and intervention implementation. She is currently president-elect for ASTD-LA.*

KNOWLEDGE IS NOT POWER; CREATIVITY IS!

Marlene Caroselli

Abstract: If knowledge *were* power, librarians would rule the world. Clearly, they do not. But the people who know how to apply the knowledge they have acquired, who know how to express the creative ideas they have in a persuasive way, can typically make a greater contribution at work than can their less imaginative colleagues.

Unfortunately, many employees in today's work force have labeled themselves as "uncreative." And yet, more than ever before, we need their creative input in order to compete in the millisecond millennium. Good ideas, well-expressed, are critically important in the new economy.

Techniques for encouraging creativity and for communicating ideas more effectively are included in this article.

CREATIVITY

Albert Einstein valued imagination above knowledge (Ghiselin, 1952). And business gurus such as Tom Peters have identified imagination as the only source of real value in today's business environment (Peters, 1992). But how do we develop in our co-workers the ability to see the big picture, to willingly propose new ideas, to break free from the mental restraints imposed by time-tested tradition?

The creative process is an incremental one. Like all harmonious efforts, it depends on a number of conditions: Good listening, tact, patience, and time for both generating possibilities and exploring their feasibility.

How can you as influencer cultivate a climate of creativity in your organization? If you've decided this is an important quality for your group to possess, you bear some responsibility for creating a climate in which new ideas can flourish. For openers, look around you for *idea toxins*—those aspects of the creativity process that may in fact be killing ideas still in their embryonic state. The toxins may be excessive pressure, lack of information, fear of ridicule, changing objectives, intimidation, and, of course, statements that stifle the creative urge. We've all heard these negative comments:

- "It'll never work."
- "Just get the job done. We don't pay you to think."
- "What makes you think your idea will work when everyone else has failed?"
- "That's the dumbest thing I've ever heard."

In building an atmosphere of receptivity, you will need to learn what is preventing ideas from being shared. Then do everything within your power to offer assurances—to make the environment one of acceptance and respect. It will help to have ground rules epitomizing the respect that hallmarks the best brainstorming sessions. For example, "No personal attacks" or "No interrupting" will encourage a full sharing of innovative possibilities.

By this stage in your influence career, you know the importance of rising above the labels (Griffith, 1990). The following people, now famous successes, were at one time all labeled as failures:

- Henry Ford went broke five times before reaching success.

- Richard Bach's classic (and best-selling) story of a seagull was rejected by eighteen publishers before finally being accepted.

- Richard Hooker's novel about the Korean War, M*A*S*H, was rejected by twenty-one publishers.

- Abraham Lincoln had numerous failures and defeats before achieving election to the presidency.

- The Duke of Wellington, a brilliant military strategist, was regarded as a dunce by his own mother.

Recognizing the danger of labeling, you are willing to take a stand if it means that creativity can be nurtured. You are aware that every great oak was once a "nut" that stood its ground. Here are additional ideas for stimulating creative thought.

1. Set Aside Time for *Brainwarming* as Well as for Brainstorming. The former activity sets the mood for the brainstorming to follow. Brainwarming is paradoxically relaxed, yet fast-paced. Characterized by humor, it nonetheless challenges your group members to put on their thinking caps. You may, for example, throw out a word as the theme for the meeting and ask for as many free-association words as the group can come up with. The brainwarmers should vary each time you meet, but they should all aim to create an atmosphere so exciting and so accepting that colleagues will jump right into the brainstorming.

During the brainstorming period, ensure that all ideas are heard and later reviewed before decisions are made or priorities are set. Remember that "creativity is not a trait monopolized by a few fortunate souls. Every person is creative, because creativity is the trait that makes us human" (Thompson, 1992, p. 4).

2. Free Thinking from the Shackles of Stereotypes. To illustrate, when asked, "How do you get to heaven?" almost every adult you ask will say something like this: "You do good deeds" or "You live by the Golden Rule." Ask a child, though, and you are likely to hear answers like these: "You take the God elevator" or "You find a beanstalk and you just keep climbing."

To stimulate this kind of thinking, ask questions like, "If money were no object, what could we accomplish here?" Better yet, compare the current state of affairs to an ideal state of affairs. Then list all the forces that could bring you closer to the ideal. In a separate column, specify the restraining forces that may be preventing you from reaching this ideal state.

3. Inject Novelty into the Thinking Process.   In order to make fullest uses of the brains you are employing, you need on occasion to push and pull, probe and prod, stimulate and scintillate. Just a little reading in the area of innovative thinking will yield an abundance of ideas. One that often works well is the "force-fit" style of thinking. You set a structure of some kind and allow a specific amount of time for meeting that challenge. On the next round, your team is asked to break its preceding record.

For example, if you were attempting to influence a group to serve as mentors for new hires, you might ask group members to list all the benefits they could think of during a three-minute period. Then, you might give them only two and one-half minutes and ask that they come up with a new list, longer if possible, but that does not contain anything already mentioned.

4. Emphasize the Value of Diversity.   It would be an unbearably boring world if we all looked alike, thought alike, sounded alike, and acted alike. Variety is not only the spice of life, it is the salt and pepper of our work day. Organizations with a diverse workforce typically have greater marketing success, a broader range of available talents and skills among their employees, and more satisfied, productive workers (Diversity Is Good Business, 1993).

Whenever you can, bring in a variety of people of differing experiences and backgrounds, ages and genders, races and religions. Further, try to mix thinking styles. It is better to combine someone with an analytical thinking style with someone who is known for creativity than to surround yourself with all convergent or all divergent thinkers. The varying viewpoints can only enhance the final product you produce.

5. When Influence Attempts Are Successful, They Almost Always Lead to Next Steps.   If you've persuaded your boss, for example, to let you attend a conference in London, you would make the obligatory report on your return. But you could do even more: You could maintain contact with other attendees and prepare a periodic update of post-conference happenings, to be shared with members of your department or organize a local conference, paralleling the most highly touted aspects of the conference in London. Or meet with your manager at the end of the year to discuss aspects of your performance that could be traced back to the growth opportunities provided by the London conference.

Although creativity is essential for improving organizations, your good ideas will not help much if you are not able to communicate them effectively.

COMMUNICATION

Stephen Covey and his associates often use the compass as a symbol to help employees find the core values or the "true north" principles that will point us in the right direction (Covey, 1994). If you are seeking good communication with and among your teammates, ideally you will be communicating a similar purity of purpose. First, though, you must define what is motivating you. It is an irreducible essence: When all else is stripped away, what is it that you stand for? That essence should come through loud and clear when co-workers think about what you have asked of them. As they communicate with one another, that essence should also undergird all their behaviors.

To work effectively with others, we must communicate effectively with others. In the words of Ned Herrmann (1996, p. 119), "The challenge for business managers is to find ways of communicating with diverse employee populations so that the intended communication actually takes place, regardless of the differences in the way people perceive." One way to meld the differences is to break down the word "communication" into its key components. To assist you in considering the effectiveness of your own communication, review the ten pairs in the following list and circle or underline the one item in each pair that you value more highly. In making your selections, ask, "Which of the two am I more likely to use?" or even "Which of the two would I rather use?"

I would rather communicate by . . .

1. arranging information chronologically OR by putting the most exciting information first

2. using familiar concepts OR by offering radical, dramatic, challenging thoughts

3. supplying familiar terms OR by exploring unknown possibilities

4. stressing a simple set of relationships OR by acknowledging the many possible cultures

5. forming strategic and new alliances OR by doing what is expected

6. expressing myself logically OR by including multiple, perhaps even contradictory, ideas

7. using statistics OR by using personal experiences/accounts

8. including data relevant to the task OR by bringing in information from a variety of sources

9. narrowing the scope OR by extending the known boundaries

10. contributing skeptical comments OR by exploring factual issues

Before we offer recommendations, there is one thing worth noting: The contingency factor. Given the complexities of circumstances, individuals, and goals, any one of these twenty items might be appropriate. Wise use of the items is contingent on sensitivity to the needs of the moment. Various circumstances demand flexibility from us; to rely repeatedly on the same communication tools is to minimize effectiveness.

But speaking in a general sense, certain elements in the communication process are effective no matter what the circumstances. You'll find those italicized in the list that follows.

1. Arranging information chronologically or putting the most exciting information first;

2. Using familiar concepts or offering radical, dramatic, challenging thoughts;

3. Supplying familiar terms or exploring unknown possibilities;

4. Stressing a simple set of relationships or *acknowledging the many possible cultures;*

5. F*orming strategic and new alliances* or doing what is expected;

6. Expressing yourself logically or *including multiple, perhaps even contradictory, ideas;*

7. Using statistics or *using personal experiences/accounts;*

8. Including data relevant to the tasks or *bringing in information from a variety of sources;*

9. Narrowing the scope or extending the known boundaries;

10. Contributing skeptical comments or exploring factual issues.

Half of the items in the ten pairs were included as "buffers." Because it is difficult sometimes to separate what we do from what we think the experts believe we should do, fifteen of the choices were included only to make the identified traits less obvious. Those fifteen are irrelevant here: Based on the author's experience and research, only the italicized five truly matter. How many of your responses match the five that are italicized?

If you had up to two matches, you have probably had some success in influencing others to join the betterment bandwagon from time to time, but there is still some room for improvement. To illustrate, although simplicity is a good thing, restricting yourself to a simplistic view may cause you to neglect the multiple possibilities embedded in the various cultures your influence project depends on. Develop your awareness of this and use the diversity of values and the value of diversity to enrich your undertaking.

If you have three matches, you're already doing an above-average job of communicating. Nonetheless, if you are the kind of person who reads self-development articles, you are the kind of person who is interested in becoming better than you presently are. For the two italicized items you are not employing, select one, and for a period of three months commit to making greater use of that particular tool. Then, for the next three-month period, concentrate on using the other.

If you had four or five matches, you probably have been told many times that you are an outstanding communicator. The number of matches confirms that fact. As an influencer, you apparently weigh the conditions in which you are influencing and select the most appropriate medium for your message. In addition, you are apparently a frequent user of the elements employed by the most able communicators.

Outstanding influencers value, and consequently demonstrate, these two traits: Innovation and communication. Their self-defined drives are aligned with the qualities employers value most. If you are determined both to gain the most from your teammates (in terms of output) and to give the most to them (in terms of input), make certain your influence exchanges reflect the best you have to offer in terms of creativity and effective communication.

CONCLUSION

No matter what your role in your organization, you can add value to projects and processes by tapping into your creative talent. It's important, of course, to recognize that you have such talent, and perhaps even more important to help others come to the same realization.

You can do this by eschewing labels and by creating an environment free of "idea toxins," an environment in which good ideas are nurtured to fruition.

But having good ideas is a necessary but not a sufficient condition for true progress. You must also be able to express those good ideas in a way that brings about positive change. Certain techniques will assist you in your idea-warrior role. Among them are demonstrating awareness of and appreciation for the diversity that surrounds you. Additionally, as a creative communicator, you will want to:

- Develop new relationships,

- Willingly explore contradictions,

- Share personal experiences, and

- Expand your references to include those from several different sources.

References

Covey, S. (1994). *First things first.* New York: Simon & Schuster.

Diversity is good business. (1993, October). *Managing Diversity, 3*(1), 5.

Ghiselin, B. (Ed.). (1952). *The creative process.* Berkeley, CA: University of California Press.

Griffith, J. (1990). *Speaker's library of business stories, anecdotes and humor.* Englewood Cliffs, NJ: Prentice Hall.

Herrmann, N. (1996). *The whole brain business book.* New York: McGraw-Hill.

Peters, T. (1992). *Liberation management.* New York: Fawcett.

Thompson, C. (1992). *What a great idea!* New York: HarperCollins.

Marlene Caroselli, Ed.D., has authored forty books (listed at the Amazon.com website). She also writes for Motivated to Sell, Stephen Covey's Excellence publications, and numerous online magazines. A popular trainer and keynote speaker, she travels extensively and writes intensively. Her expertise lies in the areas of communication, creativity, and management. Principled Persuasion: Influencing with Integrity, Selling with Standards is her most recent book, named a Director's Choice by Doubleday Book Club.

The Toolmaking Business: A New Arena for Performance Technologists

*Shonn R. Colbrunn, Michelina (Micki) Juip,
and Darlene M. Van Tiem*

Abstract: Performance technologists often seek new
ways to improve worker and organizational performance. Training is expensive and may be inconvenient
for workers to schedule and attend. Performance support, such as three-dimensional tools, offers the opportunity for immediate performance improvement.
Tools enable individuals to gain confidence, experience less frustration, reduce mistakes or uncertainty,
and accomplish desired tasks with less effort.

This article discusses the value of tools as a means
to support performance. It looks at issues related to
tool design, including usability; tool development
and construction, including selection of production
facilities, issues of manufacturability, cost, and product testing; and business considerations, including
protecting intellectual property and health and safety
during and as a result of tool usage.

INTRODUCTION

"Performance technology is a set of methods and processes for solving problems—or realizing opportunities—related to the performance of people" (Rosensweig & Newman, 1997). Performance technologists utilize a systematic approach to increase productivity, performance, and competence in the workplace. As this approach to performance improvement continues to gain momentum in organizations today, the products and services that have resulted have become incredibly diverse (Hutchison & Stein, 1998). Performance technology interventions can take the form of software systems, websites, advertising campaigns, and process diagrams. Because these interventions focus on actual performance rather than on simulated performance in training, they are both relevant and impactful.

One type of performance technology intervention often overlooked is the "tool"—a three-dimensional device that provides information to improve performance. In this article, we will present examples of performance tools used in everyday situations. In addition, we will share some of the things we learned first-hand regarding design, development, and business issues in the toolmaking business.

PERFORMANCE TOOLS

Performance tools are a type of performance support intervention. In general, performance support interventions are techniques or guides used to support the performer during the performance of a task. When we think of performance support, we often think of job aids—written or graphic reference guides that assist a person in performing certain actions such as using computer software shortcut keys or hyperlinked words that provide definitions or simple explanations (Gordon, 1994; Kemp, Morrison, & Ross, 1996; Rosensweig & Newman, 1997).

When the concept of a job aid is combined with a three-dimensional device, a wide range of performance tools is available. Performers can be supported or assisted by tools such as an engineering pocket calculator used to provide formulas for determining dimensions and calculating tolerances for quality checks of manufacturer parts. Mechanics use hand-held diagnostic devices that plug into cars just below the steering column and help identify problems. Personal digital assistants are used to store phone numbers and personal schedules and notes.

One of the most promising reasons to use performance tools is to reduce errors. Because humans are prone to making mistakes, it is helpful to design ways to eliminate or reduce them (Juran, 1992). The process of identifying errors and improving processes to eliminate errors is known as *poka-yoke* (Shingo, 1986). Shingo explains, "Whenever I hear supervisors warning workers to pay more attention or to be sure not to forget anything, I cannot help thinking that the workers are being asked to carry out operations as if they possessed divine infallibility. Rather than that approach, we should recognize that people are, after all, only human and, as such, they will on rare occasions inadvertently forget things. It is more effective to incorporate a checklist—i.e., a poka-yoke—into the operation so that if a worker forgets something, the device will signal that fact, thereby preventing defects from occurring. This, I think, is the quickest road leading to attainment of zero defects" (p. 45). In fact, Ishikawa (1985) believed that a zero-defects initiative without performance tools would be likely to fail.

CHANGE SUPPORT

Performance tools are sometimes essential to minimizing the expected learning curve for applying new skills or knowledge. "All changes require learning-curve time, and when employees are allowed to incorporate the new knowledge of change into their own pace (ideally, at a slightly faster-than-comfortable pace), the transition from what used to be to what should be will occur more easily. The results will be more deeply ingrained" (Caroselli, 1991, p. 303). Tools help shorten the learning curve by allowing performers to access relevant information when they need it on the job.

Touch-pad/Palm-Pilot-type technology and wireless technology can be used to create methods to remind people and to monitor performance. For example, hotel housekeeping staff could take advantage of this technology. Housekeeping workers come from diverse backgrounds. For some, it is difficult to read or speak English. Touch-pad tools, similar to FedEx note pads, can be created to monitor cleaning tasks or notify maintenance of room problems. Icons, similar to the hamburger and fries icons on fast food ordering pads, can be used to indicate completion of beds, bathrooms, or vacuuming.

Icons could also indicate a need to change a light bulb or check a leaky toilet. Wireless technology would allow instant status reports to identify cleaning bottlenecks. In addition, front desk attendants would know immediately when a room was ready for new occupancy.

Another example of a performance support tool comes from the authors' experience with diabetes education. Many diabetics become frustrated trying to learn about what they should eat. Part of their frustration involves shopping for foods. In the program with which we were involved, people with diabetes frequently stated that it was difficult for them to read labels and identify foods that were consistent with their meal plan. Because this was such a difficult task, many people gave up trying and selected more familiar foods, even though they were not the best choices. An instructional job aid was designed to help people with diabetes to select foods in the grocery store that fit into their meal plans.

After performing a needs analysis, we determined that a job aid would be more appropriate than additional in-depth training, as we were trying to meet an expressed need requiring performance enhancement in many different physical places. Further analysis of the situational requirements indicated that the job aid should take the form of a "tool"—a three-dimensional object that people handle and manipulate in day-to-day situations.

Our job aid was intended to make a difficult task easier by enhancing the ability of people with diabetes to self-manage their meal plans. It was not meant to be used without instruction, but rather as an adjunct to basic meal plan instruction provided during a diabetes education program. Because it was necessary for most people to shop for their own food, the tool had to make the shopping trip easier and less frustrating, while at the same time reinforcing the basics of a well-balanced meal plan.

The job aid began as a reference sheet, a very traditional idea. However, our job aid gradually developed into a notebook-like tool with moving parts. Through this experience, we learned that there are many issues related to "tool" design that we had not faced before as designers of traditional training materials.

DESIGN CONSIDERATIONS

Usability is an attribute of the way in which a particular person and system interact (Maguire, 1997). Traditionally, this field of practice has been a concern for ergonomics engineers, as in the design of manufacturing equipment and processes. In addition, usability principles have been widely researched and applied in software development for screen layout and design. However, usability is also a key consideration when designing performance improvement tools and job aids.

Donald Norman (1990) presents a number of design principles that performance technologists can apply when designing any type of object. A design should:

- Make it easy to determine what actions are possible at any moment;
- Make it easy to evaluate the current state of the system; and
- Follow natural mappings between actions and results.

In short, the designer should ensure that the user can figure out what to do and what is going on.

For our meal-planning tool, we addressed usability by anticipating challenges and designing for the intended use of the product. Because our tool was intended for use while shopping for groceries, we determined that the information should be easy to interpret at a glance. Instead of displaying a chart of data, we reformatted the data on an adjustable pull-out tab mechanism that would display only the desired information. In addition, we designed the tool to have an attached pad of paper for writing grocery lists or notes prior to the shopping experience.

DEVELOPMENT AND CONSTRUCTION

Production Facilities

Our next challenge was to find a place that could produce our tool. As training developers, we already had a list of printing shops that we had worked with on many occasions to produce paper-based materials. In addition, we had always been able to use any local copy machine as a contingency plan. However, we learned that, in the tool business, your only option is to find a production shop that can manufacture your tool.

As we researched production options, we learned that some printing shops had the ability to produce our tool by outsourcing the mechanical components. This issue is a challenge in the development of tools. The key is to be creative, so consult with people outside of your business to find production and marketing companies that may help meet your needs.

Manufacturability and Cost Issues

When we prepare paper-based training materials, our main manufacturing and cost concerns are whether or not we want our participant materials spiral bound or in a three-ring binder, black-and-white or color. With the development of tools, the complexity increases greatly.

We took our "mock-up" design to three different manufacturers in hopes of identifying the best option for a prototype and to identify a cost factor. The first manufacturer provided us with four different prototypes that we were able to test. Three prototypes had our original pull-out tab design, but with different outer packaging materials (paper, vinyl, and leather). The fourth prototype used a wheel-dial mechanism instead of a pull-out tab to display the reference information. The cost for each style differed greatly due to the difference in materials and mechanisms.

The second manufacturer, recommended by one of our financial backers, never did produce what they promised, even though we allowed them ample time. Through networking, we heard about and tried a third manufacturer. Our search for a manufacturer taught us some very valuable lessons:

- Never give your only mock-up/prototype away without a protection clause that says that if the prototype is destroyed the manufacturer will create a new one at no charge. Additionally, be certain that it is returned to you via an overnight service.

- Provide all manufacturing sources with the same initial design concept, rather than providing them with a mock-up or prototype. Our first manufacturer was the only one with any originality.

- Protect your idea and design by not letting others use your mock-up/prototype.

- Identify a date by which the manufacturer has to have a design back to you. Valuable time was lost as we waited for one design concept, which never materialized.

The third manufacturer helped us with marketability by suggesting that, if we were to sell the tool, we should give a certain percentage of the profit to a charitable organization (in this case, the American Diabetes Association) as a goodwill gesture. We were also given some ideas on how to produce the prototype in a large quantity, yet be able to satisfy small account needs. In this case, the manufacturer allowed us to print various customer logos on small batches of the tools as part of a large quantity order. Thus we were able to take advantage of the efficiencies of scale and still meet our customers' needs.

Product Testing

To test and validate our tool, we took an approach similar to the validation for an instructional job aid. We focused on validating both usability and effectiveness in supporting performance by piloting the tool with potential users (Gordon, 1994).

This performance aid was intended to be used in various settings, so users wanted something that could easily be carried in a purse or a pocket. The initial design had a pull-out tab, but user testing determined that the best design was a wheel that could be dialed to the correct information, thereby assisting with decision making on the spot. This design option was the one with the highest per unit cost, but we felt that usability was a key factor.

This job aid was also shown to the medical director in charge of resident training for the diabetes education program. He saw the potential for its use with this group of professionals in helping them educate their patients. His recommendation was to design one that was a little more upscale, that is, one with a leather exterior. Both the professional group and people with diabetes liked the pad of paper included with the tool, which could be used to keep a shopping list or notes.

In addition to evaluating the style preferences of the users, we also wanted to test the usefulness of the product for those people who had basic meal planning instruction through the diabetes education program and those who did not. The people who had participated in the program felt the tool was easy to use and met the objective of assisting them with their food selection. For those who did not have prior meal planning instruction, there was a small amount of confusion exhibited when the numbers on food labels did not fit into the ranges identified on the tool. After minimal guidance was provided, these users also said that the tool would be very useful to them. This validated our original speculation that the tool would be best used in conjunction with formal instruction.

One challenge we faced in testing was that we did not have a large supply of tools to test. Due to production economies of scale, it was not financially practical to produce a batch of our tools for testing. Instead, we had to use our prototypes and test with small numbers of users.

Business Considerations

Protecting Intellectual Property

In the field of instructional design, the standard practice for protecting print-based materials is through the use of copyright statements (for example, © 2000, Company Name) and copyright registration. However, you will need to obtain a *patent* for tools such as ours.

According to the U.S. Patent and Trademark Office (USPTO), a patent provides legal protection for any person who "invents or discovers any new and useful process, machine, manufacture, or composition of matter, or any new and useful improvement thereof" (1999). The other protection option, the trademark, is intended only for names, symbols, or devices that are used to indicate the source of goods and to distinguish them from the goods of others.

Obtaining a patent is much more complex than simply copyrighting print materials. First, the application fee for patents ranges from $400 to $500. Second, it is highly recommended that you work with an experienced patent lawyer. Third, a search of the database at the Scientific and Technical Information Center of the Patent and Trademark Office in Arlington, Virginia, must be conducted to make sure your invention/tool does not duplicate an already existing patented product. Finally, the whole process takes at least four months. Although these things may deter you from making the effort, you should be aware that patenting is the only way to protect your business interests as you market and distribute your tool. On the bright side, the USPTO website (*http://www.uspto.gov*) is a very helpful resource for information and details on obtaining a patent.

Health and Safety Issues

When developing tools, it is important to consider any potential threats to the health or safety of the user. In some situations, this may require changes in design or the addition of warning labels or statements. For example, the tool identifies the limits of sodium intake as 250 mg. for a snack and 500 mg. for an entrée. If a person followed these guidelines and had an untoward effect (increase in blood pressure, edematous extremities, and so forth), we wanted to protect ourselves from any legal claim. To accomplish this, we placed a disclaimer on the product, which reads as follows:

> "To be used as a guideline only. Meal planning should always be done under the supervision of a qualified health care provider. Calcula-

tions are approximate and meant only to indicate a range; no guarantees are implied or expressed."

Having a disclaimer on the performance aid made clear the expectations of the tool, the designers, and the user.

SUMMARY

Through our experience thus far, we have gained a great deal of insight related to designing and developing a three-dimensional tool as a performance improvement intervention, namely:

Tips for Toolmakers

- Design for usability, not cost.
- Be creative in finding production resources.
- Safeguard your ideas and product prototypes.
- Conduct real usage testing.
- Be aware of potential liabilities

Although the goal and intent are largely the same as for a traditional job aid, the complexity related to design and development and other business issues increases with a tool such as ours. We will continue to explore new areas related to marketing, pricing, and distribution of our tool. After all, exploring new areas is becoming a standard activity in the field of performance technology.

References

Caroselli, M. (1991). *Total quality transformations: Optimizing missions, methods, and management.* Amherst, MA: HRD Press.

Gordon, S.E. (1994). *Systematic training program design.* Englewood Cliffs, NJ: Prentice Hall.

Henderson, H.A., & Twerski, A.D. (1997). *Products liability problems and process* (3rd ed.). New York: Aspen.

Hutchison, C.S., & Stein, F.S. (1998). A whole new world of interventions: The performance technologist as integrating generalist. *Performance Improvement, 37,* 5, 18–25.

Ishikawa, K. (1985). *What is total quality control? The Japanese way*. Englewood Cliffs, NJ: Prentice Hall.

Juran, J.M. (1992). *Juran on quality by design*. New York: Free Press.

Kemp, J.E., Morrison, G.R., & Ross, S.M. (1996). D*esigning effective instruction*. New York: Merrill.

Maguire, M.C. (1997, May 15). *Basic usability definitions*. European Usability Support Centres. http://info.lut.ac.uk/research/husat/inuse/basicdefinitions.html (5 Aug. 1999).

Norman, D. (1990). *Design of everyday things*. New York: Doubleday.

Rosensweig, F., & Newman, C. (1997, May). The performance technology approach to performance improvement. *PRIME*, (2). http://www.med.unc.edu/intrah/prime/perfimp_doc1.html (2 Aug. 1999).

Shingo, S. (1986). *Zero quality control: Source inspection and the Poka-Yoke system*. Cambridge, MA: Productivity Press.

U.S. Patent and Trademark Office. (1999, August 5). *http://www.uspto.gov*   •

Shonn R. Colbrunn *is a performance consultant for MSX International, an engineering and business services provider based in Auburn Hills, Michigan. For the past three years he has worked onsite at Ford Motor Company and Visteon Automotive Systems providing instructional design, project management, and technology-based training expertise. Mr. Colbrunn received a bachelor's degree in psychology from Hope College and a master's degree in adult instruction and performance technology from the University of Michigan-Dearborn. He is an active member of the Michigan Chapter of ISPI.*

Michelina (Micki) Juip *is a registered nurse who has specialized in diabetes education for the past eighteen years. Ms. Juip has coordinated diabetes education programs at St. Joseph Mercy Hospital in Pontiac, Michigan, and DMC Sinai-Grace Hospital in Detroit, Michigan, and is presently manager of the Clinical Diabetes Education Program at Hurley Medical Center in Flint, Michigan. The Michigan Organization of Diabetes Educators (MODE) named Ms. Juip as its 1999 Diabetes Educator of the Year, and she was also a finalist in the American Association of Diabetes Educators (AADE) Diabetes Educator of the Year award for 1999. Ms. Juip has published many articles and spoken frequently on the topic of diabetes education. She received her BSN from the University of Michigan-Ann Arbor and is currently in the process of completing a master's degree in adult instruction and performance at the University of Michigan-Dearborn.*

Darlene M. Van Tiem is an assistant professor in the School of Education at the University of Michigan-Dearborn. She was previously the HR training director at Ameritech (Michigan, Ohio, Indiana, and Wisconsin) and curriculum manager for General Motors' technical curriculum. She received the ASTD National Technical Trainer of the Year award in 1992 and the ASTD National Excellence in Leadership award for her work with the automotive industry. Dr. Van Tiem has presented at numerous national and international conferences. She co-authored a chapter for ASTD's Technical Training Handbook, *authored a chapter for the supplement, and co-authored two ISPI books:* Fundamentals of Performance Technology *(2000) and* Performance Improvement Interventions *(in press).*

LEADING E-LEARNING

Brooke Broadbent

Abstract: The purpose of this article is to examine the
meaning and implications of e-learning and to assist
individuals and organizations, whether schools or
workplaces, with implementing e-learning. The author explains his broad definition of e-learning, discusses pros and cons of e-learning, and elaborates
ways to lead e-learning through championing, clear
communication, and effective project management.
The article contains information for leaders in education and training—instructional designers, developers, consultants, instructors, and administrators

INTRODUCTION

E-commerce, e-business, e-solutions, and now *e-learning.* What's it all about? Are these just trendy words, or do they point to new lifestyles and a new economy? Is e-learning just another new training technology that will be replaced by something "better," another flavor-of-the-month approach to training and education? Or is this a new word to describe a new reality? What does it mean to add an "e" to the word learning? As a result of being new and intrinsically vague, e-learning has generated various definitions. Elliott Masie, one of the leaders in the e-learning field (*www.smartforce.com*), tells us that the e stands for experience. The resources section on the SmartForce website explains that e-learning is dynamic, collaborative, individual, and comprehensive, that it happens in real time and enables the enterprise. Cisco tells us that e-learning is Internet-enabled learning (*www.cisco.com*). Click2learn.com takes a wide view, suggesting that e-learning refers to the creation, delivery, and management of training (*www.click2learn.com*).

I view the moniker e-learning broadly. It represents convergence in the education, training, and information fields. As I see it, the term e-learning groups together education, training, and structured information delivered by computers through the Internet, the Web, from the hard drive of the computer, or from an organization's network. This definition of e-learning includes computer-based training (CBT), web-based training (WBT), electronic performance support systems (EPSS), webcasts, listservs, and other discussions on the Internet, threaded and unthreaded.

Educators and trainers are in similar waters as they wade into the e-learning sea. They face similar challenges (even sharks), and they have much to learn from one another. Doers and thinkers in both training and education—and we need both—can sink or swim depending on the quality of their decisions and their actions. Educators and trainers facing similar challenges can help one another stay afloat. Swimming is safer when you use the buddy system.

Some thought leaders and marketers are positioning e-learning as a panacea. This is misleading. E-learning is not a universal solution. It is complex. It demands new understanding, new leadership. To assist you in acquiring the necessary knowledge to became a leader in e-learning, this article will first present the strengths and weaknesses of e-learning. Next it will consider what is required to champion e-learning in an organization, and it will conclude with several tips on how to implement e-learning successfully.

PROS AND CONS OF E-LEARNING

There are over two dozen advantages of e-learning as seen from the perspective of learners, instructors, developers, and administrators. These advantages are listed below, followed by a review of the eight issues or challenge associated with e-learning.

Ten Advantages of E-Learning for Learners

> "When I study online, there is no sitting in the back of the class. The instructor forces us to participate. It is more work than other courses. But I learn more."　　　　—George, an e-learning student

Learners appreciate the following ten qualities of e-learning:

- E-learning fosters interaction among students and instructors, which stimulates understanding and the recall of information.
- It accommodates different learning styles and fosters learning through a variety of activities that apply to different learning styles.
- It fosters self-paced learning whereby students can learn at the rate they prefer.
- It is convenient for students to access any time, any place.
- It reduces travel time and travel costs for students.
- It encourages students to browse through hyperlinks to sites on the World Wide Web and thereby find information relevant to their personal situations.
- It allows students to select learning materials or to be directed to content that meets their level of knowledge, interest, and what they need to know to perform more effectively in their particular activity.
- It provides context-sensitive help (electronic performance support systems) to computer users and helps them complete tasks on-the-fly.

- It helps users learn about the Internet, information that will help learners throughout their careers.
- It encourages students to take responsibility for their learning. Their success builds self-knowledge and self-confidence.

Seven Advantages of E-Learning for Instructors

> "I like the fact that I don't need to commute to school for classes. That way I can devote more time to my students."
> —Jane, an e-learning instructor

Instructors value the following strengths of e-learning:

- E-learning permits instructors to develop materials using the extensive resources of the Web.
- It allows instructors to communicate information in a more engaging fashion than in text-based distance education programs. E-learning offers a wide range of text, diagrams, and images with video and sound, including virtual reality technology.
- It is convenient for instructors to access any time, any place.
- It allows instructors to package essential information for all students to access. Instructors can then concentrate on high-level activities.
- It retains records of discussion and allows for later reference through the use of threaded discussion on bulletin boards.
- It generates more personal gratification for instructors through quality student participation.
- It reduces travel and accommodation costs associated with training programs.

Five Advantages of E-Learning for Instructional Developers

> "When I set up my online course, all the course information is in one place. I don't need to worry about making handouts for various classes. It is all on the Web, for anyone to access, any time, anywhere."
> —Charles, online learning developer

Advantages of e-learning experienced by instructional developers include the following:

- Developers can develop training that demonstrates, in very specific details, how to perform a task such as repairing equipment.
- E-learning sets a framework for standardized course delivery.
- E-learning makes it easier to modify training and education materials.
- E-learning allows developers to design once and use the same module in several programs by using template-like learning objects.
- E-learning promotes the orderly layout of course materials, assignments, and general administration through a Website.

Five Advantages of E-Learning for Administrators

> "We have instructors retiring in the next few years. Capturing their expertise in an online learning program will help to ensure that we don't lose their expertise." —William, a training administrator

Advantages of e-learning for training and education administrators include the following:

- E-learning accommodates automated, continuous assessment of student progress.
- Capital costs associated with traditional brick and mortar schools and training facilities are reduced.
- E-learning can be accessed by a variety of platforms such as Windows, UNIX, and MAC because they are all html-compatible.
- The template approach to developing online learning engenders consistency.
- Institutions can build the e-learning modules from courses of leading instructors.

Eight Issues with E-Learning

> "When I started to develop e-learning I had no help. I wish I had taken the time to learn about all the resources that exist."
> —Allan, teacher of e-learning

All is not rosy on the e-learning front. There are challenges, issues—optimists might call them opportunities—to address. Issues associated with the use of e-learning are as follows:

- Students may be required to purchase or rent new computer equipment.

- Technical difficulties or operator error may hamper students and instructors.

- Students and instructors may have gaps in their computer knowledge, so they will require training in computer basics before they can start the on-line training.

- Using telephones lines and Internet service providers to access the Internet, when required, leads to high user fees in many parts of the world.

- Initial costs of developing courses may be considerable, depending on the approach taken.

- Instructors may need to become familiar with electronic textbooks, Internet-based research material, copyright, and other e-learning related topics.

- Internet bandwidth may not be robust enough to support the desired level of multimedia.

- People working in the e-learning field at an individual location may be pioneers and not have the support of a network of more experienced colleagues.

Our quick review of the pros and cons tends to underscore the diversity of e-learning. The challenge one faces as an e-learning leader is to reap the benefits and avoid the pitfalls. What can a leader do to achieve success with e-learning? One of the first steps is to become an effective champion.

ARE YOU A CHAMPION?

> "E-learning has many facets. From initial leadership through development and evaluation, you need strong people at the helm to succeed."
>   —E-learning manager

Have you ever championed a cause? Maybe it was at school, in your community, at church, or at work. You believed in something and stated your support. You tried to bring others to see issues and events as you saw them. How did it go? What went well? What would you do differently next time?

Leaders who know their subject well and express themselves clearly become effective champions. Successful champions—instructional designers, developers, consultants, instructors, and administrators—help ensure successful implementation of e-learning. The following material will give you a chance to reflect on effective strategies for championing a cause and give you some tips about explaining e-learning to stakeholders.

The Role of Champions

Champions play important roles in helping organizations understand new ideas. A champion must have in-depth knowledge of the ideas he or she is advocating. Also, a champion must understand the preoccupations of the persons who are receiving the message. Champions must communicate effectively with a planned approach.

Know Your Subject

Take every opportunity you can to expand your knowledge of e-learning. At the same time, think critically about the information that comes your way. You will find free and reputable newsletters and articles about e-learning at The Masie Center (*www.masie.com*), Brandon Hall's Website (*www.brandon-hall.com*), and the e-learning portal I launched called e-LearningHub.com. In addition, ASTD publishes a robust online magazine called *Learning Circuits*. *Inside Technology Training* is another excellent magazine about e-learning topics, available in a hard copy or electronically.

Another way to learn about e-learning is to take a course, teach one, or develop one. There are modest, but free courses available at Virtual University (*www.vu.org*). Or you could teach a course at Virtual University or set up a course at any of a number of virtual classrooms such as Blackboard (*www.blackboard.go.com*), eSocrates (*www.esocrates.com*), FirstClass (*www.softarc.com*), click2learn (*www.click2learn*), and WebCT (*www.WebCT.com*). There are several good books about e-learning, and many of these are reviewed at e-LearningHub.com.

Know Your Stakeholders

If you are championing e-learning, chances are your stakeholders will have some areas of concern or "hot spots." If you identify these hot spots and address them, it will be easier to lead an e-learning project. The list below summarizes the hot spots of managers and administrators in business and education today.

- The bottom-line focus of modern business leads training managers to seek ways to reduce training program costs.

- Reduced funding for education and training has forced institutions to look for more economical ways to deliver education.

- On campus and at training centers, the pressures on space, teaching time, and facilities such as laboratories and libraries lead to an openness to consider alternative delivery methods.

- The expanding number of mature students are motivated, independent learners and are ready for the independent study mode of e-learning.

- Many full-time and part-time students are under economic pressures, work part-time, and appreciate the reduced travel time of e-learning.

- Our entrepreneurial society is preoccupied with proving that it produces quality products. E-learning, with interactive Internet communication tools, is certainly an improvement over traditional distance education.

- Entrepreneurs look at the forecasts for huge growth in the number of North Americans using online learning. Many of these users will be employed full-time and studying part-time. To investors, they represent an attractive market. Most have college degrees and good incomes, and it seems they will be ready to spend their money to study online.

- Full-time students and part-time students who are working full-time and leading harried lives appreciate the opportunity to study from the comfort of their homes and avoid commuting to a campus.

Deal with Skepticism

When approaching stakeholders with a proposal for e-learning, an advocate of e-learning should bear in mind that the stakeholders might be skeptical about technological innovation. This skepticism might stem from involvement in a failed information technology implementation or from another negative experience. An effective champion anticipates the resistance of stakeholders and develops counterarguments.

Here are a few facts and figures you should be familiar with when you are talking to other people about e-learning. Essentially, the message is that computer projects can be far more complex than one anticipates. They can cost far more money than planned and take far more time. Also, computer projects tend to generate unanticipated post-implementation costs. Moreover, we will see below that some university professors have specific concerns with e-learning.

The stakeholders you try to convince about e-learning might not be familiar with the sources we cite below, but chances are that they have been part of a computer project that did not deliver as planned. Therefore they might approach your e-learning proposals with guarded optimism—or skepticism.

In the mid-1990s the Standish Group found that only 16.2 percent of software projects are completed on time and on-budget (standishgroup.com). *Scientific American* reported in 1997 that the bill for supporting computers far exceeds initial expenditures. For example, the average annual bill for supporting each computer was in the neighborhood of $13,000, including technical support, service technicians, and time wasted when systems are down (*www.scientificamerican.com*). *Technorealism* points out that we should both fear and welcome new technology. Most of all, we need to be realistic. *Technorealism* articulates eight principles for thinking critically about technology and approaching it realistically (*www.technorealism.org*).

Some faculty members have real concerns about technology and on-line learning. Professor David Noble argues that the trend toward automation of higher education is a battle between students and professors on one side, and university administrations and companies with "educational products" to sell (firstmonday.dk). Professor Andrew Feenberg was an online learning innovator. Today he sees politicians, university administrations, and computer and telecommunications companies taking over from faculty. This commercial approach, in his mind, is guaranteed to provoke instant hostility among faculty (*www.aaup.org*).

We can see that there are legitimate sources of skepticism about IT projects and, by projection, their little cousins—e-learning projects. The important idea here is to be aware that others might be far less enthusiastic about e-learning than you are as a project leader. In general, one of the most effective actions you can take to overcome opposition to e-learning is to make certain that you communicate effectively.

Communicate Effectively

An effective champion achieves success through clear communication. It is hard to explain new things to people when they know nothing about them. Have you ever tried to talk to people about technology-assisted learning? Did they look confused? Did they look away when you tried to engage them? Perhaps they pretended they understood. But did they? Here are some thoughts about communicating clearly, engaging your listeners, and championing a cause—such as e-learning.

My good friend, Paul Corkum, is a scientist. It seems that every time I see him, he is just returning from an international scientific conference at which he has presented a provocative paper about a new scientific discovery to do with ultrafast-pulse lasers. When I ask Paul about his latest research, he grabs the nearest prop and eases into a jargon-free story. Recently, for example, he pulled the pen out of his shirt pocket and started to explain to me how his lab has managed to use a laser to rotate molecules.

I know precious little about physics. My academic background is in history and education. So it is a miracle that Paul can explain to me, a scientific ignoramus, the latest scientific discoveries. I suspect that Paul loves the challenge and accepts it willingly. He smiles through his explanation. He always tells me what practical applications his research might lead to, how it could affect me personally one day. He uses props. He uses simple words. He does not talk down. He makes me feel good about our interaction. With his enthusiasm, vast knowledge, and willingness to come to my level, Paul engages me in another one of his moments in the history of science. I feel privileged. And I learn something! Even better—I retain what he tells me. Months later my mind's eye clearly evokes the image of Paul talking to me.

There are lessons here that apply to explaining and championing e-learning. You can use Paul's approach with colleagues, managers, stakeholders, and sponsors. All of these people need to understand e-learning. What you say is important. How you say it is even more important. People who surround you need to understand e-learning in order to support you and your e-learning projects. However, these key stakeholders might be as ignorant of e-learning as I am of physics. By following Paul's example you will communicate better about e-learning and become a more effective champion.

A Phone-In Radio Show

To appreciate the challenge of explaining e-learning, think of yourself as an "expert" on a one-hour radio phone-in show about e-learning. If you cannot imagine yourself doing a radio phone-in show, then choose another scenario that seems realistic to you. Perhaps you are explaining e-learning to a management group or friends at a party or to a neighbor.

The first question from the host of the radio show, or the one that is probably on the minds of other people you talk to, will be something like, "What is e-learning?" Remember when you answer not to use jargon and to be enthusiastic. On the radio you must be concise and precise. You can hook your listeners if you mention the potential impact of e-learning on them. Pretend your listeners know precious little about e-learning. Maybe they don't know much about technology. However, they have all attended a school, so you can use schools as a point of departure.

Your answer might be something like the following: E-learning is a way to teach. It replaces or supplements brick and mortar schools and training centers with a computer. There are three elements of e-learning: (1) A learner; (2) technology, including a computer; and (3) information or skills to be learned. E-learning is important to each of us because it offers a new way to learn any place, any time.

Did I succeed? Was my explanation free of jargon and enthusiastic? Did I describe the potential impact of e-learning on my listeners? What would you change for your audience? Maybe your audience is familiar with CBT. In that case you should explain that CBT is included in our definition of e-learning. And you could go on to explain what online learning has that CBT does not have and what CBT has that e-learning does not have. If your audience is sophisticated, you could explain that e-learning is an appropriate term because it combines different approaches to learning. Computer-based training is merging with Web-based training and EPSS, and the Internet is being used to support discussions among students and instructors.

Avoid Confusing E-Learning Jargon

When I talk with colleagues or savvy clients about e-learning, we sometimes use terms that our stakeholders either do not know or do not know very well. When e-learning experts talk to stakeholders, they must be careful to avoid using jargon that stakeholders will not understand. If champions use jargon, they risk confusing or alienating stakeholders. "Asynchronous" is a fine word with the right crowd, as is "distributed learning." But when we use such terms with people who do not know them, we tend to drive a wedge between ourselves and those people.

If you have been using some of these terms for so long that they roll off your tongue and you have trouble finding substitutes, look for simple explanations. For example, synchronous communication can be called "real time" communication or "immediate" communication. You can explain that synchronous communication is analogous to using the telephone.

Different Communication Strokes for Different Folks

Effective communication will help to gain understanding and acceptance of your e-learning program. In order to be effective, you must develop a communication strategy. To do that, collect your thoughts around the following:

1. Which groups have to know about the e-learning program?

2. What message does each group have to hear?

3. What do they not have to hear?

4. When should the message go to them?

5. How should the message be distributed?

6. Who should be associated with the message as a spokesperson?

7. Who should not deliver the message?

8. What are my skills for delivering the message?

9. Where do I require assistance to deliver the championing message?

10. Who can help when I require assistance to deliver the championing message?

11. How should I approach people who can help me?

After you and your team have answered the questions above (and any others, based on your environment), you might decide that the best way to communicate with one group is a short message from senior management. With another group, the best way could be to make short presentations during regularly scheduled meetings. And you might also decide to craft an interesting, people-oriented article in the organization's newsletter. For each of these efforts to communicate about e-learning, you will need to develop messages that deal with the specific concerns of the individual target groups.

Managing an E-Learning Project

> "Don't forget that organizations are made up of people. People resist change. You have to deal with their resistance when you introduce e-learning."   —Comment from an e-learning administrator

If you—instructional designers, developers, consultants, instructors, and administrators—do help introduce e-learning in your organization, you will probably be fostering substantive change. Introducing e-learning in an organization changes the way students learn, and it could change the roles of everyone associated with learning. It is no wonder you may experience considerable resistance. E-learning normally means using the Web, CBT, and EPSS instead of attending classes and it's an adjustment—especially for learners. Use a wide range of thoughtful tactics to create a positive environment for introducing e-learning. The following guidelines help to get results from e-learning:

Four Tips for Starting an E-Learning Project

1. *Use the correct e-learning terminology.* Teach it to others and encourage them to learn the correct terms. A shared language will help people to understand what e-learning is and to communicate with one another.

2. *Encourage frank discussion.* We need to create a safe place for opposing ideas to be expressed. Better to bring them out and to try to deal with conflicting ideas than to force them underground, where they will fester.

3. *Be creative.* There is no one way to do e-learning. Online learning does not need to be an all-or-nothing phenomenon. You can combine e-learning with leader-led instruction.

4. *Promote the concept.* You will know that stakeholders are ready for e-learning when they are ready to take the time to talk to you. Exploit these opportunities when they occur and positively report on your progress.

Three Tips for Communicating About E-Learning

1. *Be decisive.* Consensus building is not good enough. When you lead an e-learning intervention, colleagues and clients will expect you to be predictable, to make decisive statements, and to keep your actions congruent with your statements.

2. *Bring issues alive.* The difference between a good e-learning project manager and a great one is that a great one makes the issues come alive for

people, creates a sense of urgency, and helps people sing from the same song sheet.

3. *Remain positive.* Most people want you to succeed. If you remain positive, think critically about what you are doing, and adjust your actions when you don't succeed, you will eventually succeed.

Three Tips for Managing E-Learning Projects

1. *Divide and conquer.* An e-learning intervention may seem daunting; however, chunked into achievable segments it is doable. Inch by inch life is a cinch, yard by yard it gets very hard!

2. *Manage expectations.* Typically at the outset of a change intervention such as the implementation of e-learning, people are enthusiastic. Later, when events don't go as well as predicted, when deadlines are missed, and when some unrealistic goals are not achieved, people may become negative. One goal of a project manager is to manage expectations. If you do not let people become overly optimistic at the beginning, then the chances are reduced that they will be in despair when all targets are not achieved.

3. *Foster teamwork.* Effective teams, with people helping each other, accomplish more than individuals. Members of effective teams place the success of the group above their individual success. E-learning leaders need to establish expectations for teamwork, model appropriate behaviors, and reward teamwork.

Four Tips for Managing Risks Associated with E-Learning Projects

1. *Sustain momentum.* Every project has potential pitfalls in such areas as time, scope, quality, and resources. Monitor these four interrelated variables, report on their status, and develop tactics to attenuate risks to the project's success.

2. *Achieve early wins.* As you implement e-learning and incur problems and opportunities, go after the low fruit, the things that are easiest to harvest. You need some early wins to show success.

3. *Deal with resistance.* A few people may resist what you are doing in e-learning. Learn about the people who are resisting and the source of their resistance. Their resistance may be well-founded. Learn whether they are unwilling, unable, or unknowing and develop appropriate strategies to address their resistance.

4. *Manage scope creep.* As e-learning projects progress, expectations of people involved in the projects may grow. Most of these expectations can

only be met by doing additional work. If you do agree to take on more than you outline in your original work plan, you must be very clear that this requires more resources or time; otherwise quality will suffer and you will miss deadlines or have to compromise some part of your project.

As an important player in the e-learning game, you will help organizations sort through the hype and see whether they are ready for e-learning. Common sense, critical thinking, and a constant focus on what needs to be done to improve employees' performance must be your beacons. If you plan your work and work your plan, you and your organization will be ready for e-learning.

SUMMARY

Implementing e-learning is not for the faint of heart. It can be challenging. You could experience setbacks, even failure. To succeed you must understand the up and down sides of e-learning. You must address the weaknesses—especially the perceptions of weaknesses or the skepticism of stakeholders. Successful champions of e-learning are effective communicators. They explain new words clearly, concretely, in terms that their listeners understand. The essence of championing is clear communication. Decide what you want to say, to whom, and how. Design a plan and follow through on it. Remember that stakeholders need answers. Effective champions anticipate questions before they are asked, find the answers, and deliver them in a convincing manner. The tips, tactics, and strategies provided in this article play a pivotal role in the successful implementation of an e-learning program. Plan the start of the project, concentrate on communicating, manage carefully, identify risks and address them, and, most of all, lead—inspire the people around you with your support for the e-learning project and with your reasoned enthusiasm.

Anchors Away!

Tempted to go sailing in the e-learning sea? Looking for a vessel? Do you see yourself as the captain, the leader? Need an anchor, charts, or navigational aids? As a first step, check out the websites cited at the end of this article.

I wish you smooth sailing!

Sources

http://blackboard.go.com/

http://firstmonday.dk/issues/issue3_1/noble/

http://ittrain.com/

http://www.aaup.org/SO99Feen.htm

http://www.asymetrix.com/solutions/online_learning.html

http://www.brandon-hall.com/

http://www.cisco.com/warp/public/10/wwtraining/elearning/elearning.html

http://www.click2learn.com/

http://www.e-learninghub.com

http://www.esocrates.com/home/educators/

http://www.learningcircuits.org/

http://www.masie.com/

http://www.scientificamerican.com/0797issue/0797trends.html

http://www.smartforce.com/corp/marketing/articles/frames_emasie.html

http://www.smartforce.com/corp/marketing/articles/frames_elearn.html

http://www.softarc.com/downloads/index.shtml

http://standishgroup.com/chaos.html

http://www.technorealism.org/overview.html

http://www.vu.org/

http://www.WebCT.com/try/

Brooke Broadbent *is an e-learning specialist working as an author, trainer, and management consultant. He is the founder of e-LearningHub.com, a website devoted to e-learning. He is the VP of Knowledge Management at Learneze.com, a full-service e-learning company. He is a frequent contributor to training publications and the author of* Using the Internet Smarter and Faster *(Crisp, 1998). He is currently writing a book about e-learning in conjunction with the American Society for Training and Development.*

How to Increase Training Effectiveness with Systems Thinking

Gary Schouborg

Abstract: Any activity is part of a system. In particular, training has three interrelated goals: (1) learning and (2) the application of that learning on the job (training transfer), so that (3) the organization meets its objectives. The author applies systems thinking to training by identifying the key contributors to training effectiveness: managers, supervisors, trainers, and trainees. The author then provides a list of activities that those contributors can do to ensure that training helps the organization meet its objectives.

KEY TASK

The key task in promoting training effectiveness is to identify organizational objectives in order to design training that will help achieve them. Systems thinking helps make the objectives sufficiently broad. For example, there are many stakeholders in an organization that training directly or indirectly impacts: owners (for-profit), sponsors or directors (not-for-profit), managers or administrators, supervisors, trainers, trainees, and (last, but certainly not least) customers or clients. Identifying training's impact on all of them has three primary advantages. It enables (1) management to provide training for optimal impact, (2) trainers to design and deliver training for optimal impact, and (3) trainees to understand the relevance of the training for their own work. This third benefit provides both direction and motivation for the trainees—first to learn and then to apply their learning effectively on the job.

There are many tools for considering a system as a whole. Figure 1 provides a model that many have found helpful. As seen in the figure, at the core of any organizational systems thinking is a dynamically interrelated triad of *customer satisfaction, organizational processes,* and *employee involvement*. The labels may differ among organizations. For example, not-for-profits may be inclined

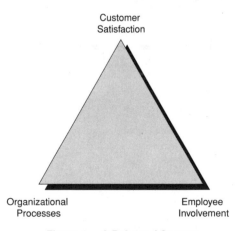

Figure 1.   A Balanced System

to refer to those they serve as "clients" rather than as customers, and to those who do the work as "members" rather than as employees. But the concepts are essentially the same for purposes of training effectiveness.

Unless *customers* are satisfied, your organization will not survive, let alone meet its objectives. Customers, however, will not be satisfied unless their requirements are met in a timely manner, at a price that is acceptable to them, and at a cost that is acceptable to your organization. (In the long run, your organization cannot continue to satisfy customers if its costs are too high. Therefore, your costs limit what customer needs you can reliably promise to meet.) To meet both customer and organizational requirements, you must continuously improve your organizational *processes*. That won't happen unless problems are addressed at levels at which they occur and where solutions are available— that is, unless *employees* are involved in improving them. Because employees are people and not just cogs in a machine, they have their own goals, which must be coordinated with those of the organization, as appropriate.

TRANSFER AS A LINCHPIN

The linchpin of effective training is *transfer*, which focuses attention on how what is learned in training will be applied to the job. Transfer encourages training to be conducted, not in isolation, but in reference to its future use. That use in turn reminds all parties that the ultimate purpose is for the organization to meet its objectives. Transfer therefore provides both direction and motivation to all stakeholders of training. It also assures that training will not just be a break from work, but an occasion for trainees to clarify their roles in the organization and renew their commitment to its goals by improving their skills.

There are several ways to promote transfer. Following are activities that different groups can do before, during, and after training. "Supervisor" here refers to the immediate boss, for example, the president is "supervisor" of the vice president; "management" refers to any management level above supervisor; and "training team" refers to anyone involved in training, from developer to instructor. Although particular groups are directly responsible for only some of the activities, higher management is involved in all of them.

The lists* are not meant to imply that you must strive to do all the activities mentioned, or even as many as possible. Rather, they are meant as a

---

*These lists were taken from a manual for evaluating training effectiveness (Schouborg, 1993). They were also based heavily on extensive work already done on transfer (Broad & Newstrom, 1992).

menu from which you can choose to optimize training effectiveness in particular circumstances.

Before Training

Management

   1. Creates an Advisory Committee

   2. Provides Executive Memo/Audio/Video

   3. Provides Supervisors with Coaching Skills

   4. Informs Supervisors of Performance Standards

   5. Minimizes Interruptions

   6. Creates Logical Work Groups

Supervisor

   7. Adopts Performance Measures

   8. Attends Orientation for Supervisors

   9. Selects Trainees

  10. Selects Logical Groups

  11. Conducts Before-Training Meeting

  12. Uses Previous Graduates

  13. Allows On-the-Job Preparation

  14. Plans for After Training

Trainee

  15. Completes Self-Assessment

  16. Completes Advance Assignment

Training Team

  17. Identifies Needs with Trainees

  18. Identifies Barriers on Job

  19. Sends Advance Letter to Supervisor

  20. Sends Advance Letter to Trainees

  21. Sends Advance Assignment

During Training

Management

1. Provides Introduction: Live/Audio/Video
2. Participates in Instruction

Supervisor

3. Sends Entire Work Group
4. Minimizes Interruptions
5. Attends with Trainees
6. Inquires into Trainee Absences

Trainee

7. Creates Personal Action Plan
8. Creates Application Notebook
9. Negotiates Applications Contract
10. Plans for Prevention from "Relapse"
11. Brings Real Project from Work
12. Picks Training/Working Buddy
13. Joins in Group Action Plan

Training Team

14. Emphasizes Positive Results of Transfer
15. Helps Trainees to Unlearn Barrier Behavior
16. Provides Job Aids
17. Simulates Work Environment
18. Provides Real Work Projects
19. Creates Support Groups

After Training

Management

1. Models Targeted Performance
2. Creates Protective Environment
3. Provides Incentive

Supervisor

4. Debriefs Trainees

5. Sets Realistic Goals

6. Creates Protective Environment

7. Provides Incentive

8. Coaches/Models

9. Provides Support Groups

10. Has Trainees Train Peers

11. Documents/Reports on Progress

Trainee

12. Sets Realistic Goals

13. Refers to Training Materials

14. Uses Buddy System

15. Uses Self-Motivation Techniques

16. Monitors Own Performance

Training Team

17. Advises Supervisor

18. Provides Follow-Up Questions/Recognition

19. Provides Follow-Up Readings/Exercises

20. Provides Refresher Course

21. Provides Advanced Training

EXPLORATION OF LISTED ITEMS

Let's explore further descriptions of the items listed.

Before Training

The following activities, when conducted before training, tend to promote the transfer of what is learned to the workplace.

Management

1. *Creates an Advisory Committee.* A management advisory committee helps ensure the relevance and effectiveness of the training program.

Systems Thinking: Management has the ultimate responsibility to keep the organization's eye on the ball. It must understand customer requirements, business processes, the level of employee involvement, and the optimal relationship among the three to achieve business objectives. Only within such a perspective can training needs be most advantageously identified and pursued.

2. *Provides Executive Memo/Audio/Video.* Sends a written memo, audiotape, or videotape to trainees and their supervisors informing them of the business purpose of prospective training.

Systems Thinking: Management's vision must be communicated clearly and be seen as coming from management itself.

3. *Provides Supervisors with Coaching Skills.* Gives supervisors training in coaching skills that will enable them to help trainees apply newly learned skills to the job.

Systems Thinking: Management would not think of purchasing capital equipment without the resources to maintain it properly; training supervisors in coaching skills is maintaining supervisors at peak operational efficiency.

4. *Informs Supervisors of Performance Standards* The performance standards for supervisors include that they be able to help trainees apply newly learned skills to the job in an effective way.

Systems Thinking: This is a case of the general systems thinking principle that standards are required for every aspect of the business so that stable processes can be identified, consistently applied, and continuously improved when desirable.

5. *Minimizes Interruptions.* This prevents trainees from being interrupted by job responsibilities while in training.

Systems Thinking: Management is responsible for creating systems that allow all resources, including humans, to operate at peak efficiency. The training system, just like any other system, must not be interrupted while it is operating if it is to achieve its purpose.

6. *Creates Logical Work Groups.* Work groups that are logically related train together. During training, such groups can more easily discuss among themselves how they can apply their learning to the job. After training, they can more easily support one another in applying their learning to the job.

Systems Thinking: Communication and cooperation among individuals and work groups is a key part of obtaining the employee participation necessary to improve performance continuously.

Supervisor

7. *Adopts Performance Measures.* The supervisor develops performance measurements by which to measure gains due to training.

Systems Thinking: Processes cannot be continuously and reliably improved unless they are measured.

8. *Attends Orientation for Supervisors.* The supervisor attends an orientation session that summarizes the training content. This improves his or her ability, after training, to assist subordinates in applying learning to the job. It also helps in doing items 9 through 11 and 14 below.

Systems Thinking: Supervisors can help increase employee participation by coaching; management can help supervisors do their jobs by providing appropriate training.

9. *Selects Trainees.* Supervisors select subordinates to attend training based on an analysis of the company's business goals, the subordinates' developmental needs, and the training objectives. The timing of the training is an important consideration.

Systems Thinking: Supervisors cannot select trainees properly unless management has clearly communicated training objectives relative to both the company's and its customers' requirements. Nor can supervisors identify the subordinates' developmental needs unless they (supervisors) have been given the time and skills necessary to communicate effectively with subordinates. Finally, supervisors cannot have people trained most effectively unless organizational processes are established that allow training to be timely (as close as possible to when the skills learned in training will be needed on the job).

10. *Selects Logical Groups.* Supervisors select work groups that are logically related to train together. During training, such groups can more easily discuss among themselves how they can apply their learning to the job. After training, they can more easily support one another in applying their learning to the job.

Systems Thinking: Build partnership and cooperation wherever it is constructive to do so. Be careful of thinking too narrowly about what groups are logically related; overcome functional and departmental barriers when appropriate.

11. *Conducts Before-Training Meeting.* Supervisors conduct meeting(s) with trainees to discuss how the training is expected to benefit the trainees and the organization.

Systems Thinking: Appropriate levels of management must communicate the goals to subordinates.

12. *Uses Previous Graduates.* Supervisors employ previous graduates of the training to prepare prospective trainees.

Systems Thinking: Although this recommendation flows directly from learning principles about modeling, systems thinking, by its emphasis on teamwork and communication, creates a climate in which management is more willing than it would otherwise be to spend the resources of previous graduates in this way and the graduates themselves are more willing than they would otherwise be to participate.

13. *Allows On-the-Job Preparation.* Supervisors allow trainees time on the job to prepare for training.

Systems Thinking: Clearly identifying "the vital few" things that must be done to improve performance and increases the likelihood that the precise importance of any targeted training will be clearly understood. This in turn promotes the attitude that whatever has to be done to support that training will be done—including time on the job to prepare for training.

14. *Plans for After Training.* Supervisors plan with trainees how they will apply their learning to the job after training.

Systems Thinking: Wherever possible, work in general (and training especially) should be planned far ahead of time to minimize errors.

Trainee

15. *Completes Self-Assessment.* The trainee uses self-assessment tools to ensure that training will meet his or her developmental needs and those of the business.

Systems Thinking: Self-assessment of all aspects of performance is essential to being constructively involved in one's work.

16. *Completes Advance Assignment.* Trainees complete any pre-training assignments. This is usually a reading or individual exercise, but it may also involve completing a work project on the job.

Systems Thinking: Work should be done when and where it can be done most cost-effectively. Some aspects of training are best done outside the formal training environment.

Training Team

17. *Identifies Needs with Trainees.* The team includes prospective trainees as participants in the needs analysis.

Systems Thinking: Encourage employee participation whenever appropriate. Encourage customer participation in needs analysis; remember that trainees are the training team's customers.

18. *Identifies Barriers on Job.* The team identifies potential barriers to the trainees being able to apply the newly learned skills to the job. The more precise the identification, the better the chance of overcoming the barrier.

Systems Thinking: Identify possible problems ahead of time and then identify and reduce potential causes. It is less costly to plan ahead than to re-work after errors have been made.

19. *Sends Advance Letter to Supervisor.* The team sends advance letters to the prospective trainees' supervisor(s) to explain the nature and expectations of the training.

Systems Thinking: Work is never dumped on anyone; it is assigned while communicating its nature and explaining how it contributes to the company objectives.

20. *Sends Advance Letter to Trainees.* The team sends advance letters to the prospective trainees to explain the nature and expectations of the training.

Systems Thinking: Work is never dumped on anyone; it is assigned while communicating its nature and explaining how it contributes to the company's objectives.

21. *Sends Advance Assignment.* The team gives any advance assignments to the prospective trainees.

Systems Thinking: Work should be done when and where it can be done most cost-effectively; some aspects of training are best done outside the formal training itself.

During Training

The following is a list of activities that can be conducted during training that tend to promote the transfer of what is learned in training to the workplace.

Management

1. *Provides Introduction: Live/Audio/Video.* Management introduces the training at the very beginning, either in person or by audiotape or videotape. The purpose should be to explain the relevance of the training to the business and how management intends to support its application back on the job. The more motivating the presentation the better.

Systems Thinking: Employees are more productive when they feel they are working with a visible, involved management team.

2. *Participates in Instruction.* Management participates in the training as instructors. The more effective the participation the better.

Systems Thinking: Encourage everyone, management as well as non-management, to participate *whenever it is feasible and productive to do so.* The presence of management in the classroom, even if only with a brief motivational introduction, signals employees that the training is important. When feasible, the more management can show knowledge of the content of the training and convey its relevance to organizational goals, the more trainees will understand the importance of what they are being asked to learn.

Supervisor

3. *Sends Entire Work Group.* The supervisor sends the entire work group to train together. This prevents untrained employees from discouraging trainee performance improvement after training.

Systems Thinking: Encourage teamwork whenever it is feasible and productive.

4. *Minimizes Interruptions.* The supervisor prevents (or at least reduces) work-related interruptions during training.

Systems Thinking: Management at the appropriate level(s) is responsible for creating systems that allow all resources, including human, to operate at peak efficiency. If it is to achieve its goals, the training system, just like any other system, must not be interrupted while it is operating. As the management level most aware of conflicts between the needs of the job and time off for training, the supervisor must help appropriate levels of management establish policies that will protect the integrity of the training process.

5. *Attends with Trainees.* The supervisor attends some of the training with the trainees.

Systems Thinking: Encourages everyone, management as well as non-management, to participate whenever it is feasible and productive to do so.

6. *Inquires into Trainee Absences.* The supervisor inquires into why the trainees were absent from any of the training.

Systems Thinking: Demands root-cause analysis of any nonperformance; does so for preventive rather than punitive reasons.

Trainee

Systems Thinking: The following activities (7 through 13) are particular instances of the general principle that employees should be involved in planning and designing their own work whenever feasible and productive.

7. *Creates Personal Action Plan.* The trainee creates a personal action plan for applying the new skill or knowledge to the job.

8. *Creates Application Notebook.* During training, the trainee creates a notebook of ideas on how what is being learned can be applied back on the job. For example, sales reps who are learning how to defuse the anger of an

unsatisfied customer might identify specific customers and detail how they would apply the training in those cases.

9. *Negotiates Applications Contract.* The trainee negotiates with his or her supervisor about specific commitments for applying back on the job what is learned in training. For example, the sales reps mentioned above might ask to have their initial efforts monitored by the supervisor or a fellow worker so they can receive constructive feedback on how effectively they are applying the training or they might negotiate a small amount of time away from customers each day so they can review the lessons to be applied. They might also commit to creating a job aid they would use while dealing with an irate customer.

10. *Plans for Prevention of "Relapse."* The trainee plans for preventing himself or herself from reverting to pre-training behavior on the job.

11. *Brings Real Project from Work.* The trainee brings a real project from the job to be worked on during training.

12. *Picks Training/Working Buddy.* The trainee picks a buddy from his or her own work unit to train with and work with in applying the new skill or knowledge to the job.

13. *Joins in Group Action Plan.* The trainee participates in creating a group action plan for his or her work group.

Training Team

Systems Thinking: The following activities (14 through 19) directly flow from learning principles. By emphasizing how different processes are interrelated within systems, however, systems thinking encourages the training team to look beyond formal training to the workplace in which what is learned will be applied.

14. *Emphasizes Positive Results of Transfer.* The training team emphasizes the positive results of the trainees' applying new skill or knowledge to the job. This may involve leading the trainees through descriptions of what the future will be after transfer has been achieved.

15. *Helps Trainees to Unlearn Barrier Behavior.* The team helps the trainees unlearn any behavior that would inhibit the transfer of new skill or knowledge to the job.

16. *Provides Job Aids.* The training team provides job aids (for example, checklists, decision tables, charts, diagrams, and reference materials) to assist recall and application.

17. *Simulates Work Environment.* The team simulates the work environment in a way that will enhance the trainees' ability to apply learning to the job.

18. *Provides Real Work Projects.* The team provides opportunities for trainees to perform real work during training.

19. *Creates Support Groups.* The team creates support groups by facilitating exchanges of contacts and information.

After Training

The following is a list of activities that can be conducted after training that tend to promote the transfer of what is learned to the workplace.

Management

1. *Models Targeted Performance.* Management models the performance that is targeted by the training.

Systems Thinking: Continuous improvement will not occur unless management is committed to it and models it. Even though there is no point to management's modeling typing skills, for example, management can promote typing training by modeling a constructive and open attitude toward appropriately improving one's own skills.

2. *Creates Protective Environment.* Management creates a protective environment for the trainees while they are first learning to apply their new knowledge, skill, or attitude. This includes giving them time to try out their new learning, limiting their risk in doing so, and providing them with the tools, supplies, and facilities necessary.

Systems Thinking: Management is responsible for creating systems that allow all resources, including human, to operate at peak efficiency. The training system, just like any other system, operates best under certain conditions that must be identified and supported.

3. *Provides Incentive.* Management encourages the trainees to apply what they have learned.

Systems Thinking: Recognizes that human beings are the key to improving business processes and therefore carefully identifies and employs the incentives that drive employees to their most productive behavior.

Supervisor

4. *Debriefs Trainees.* The supervisor debriefs the trainees to find out what happened in training and how they expect that to impact their jobs.

Systems Thinking: Processes must be continuously monitored to determine whether they are meeting standards. Employees should participate in monitoring performance and setting standards whenever feasible and productive.

5. *Sets Realistic Goals.* The supervisor sets realistic goals for the trainees in transferring to the job what they learned in training.

Systems Thinking: Processes must be identified and stabilized before performance goals can be realistically established.

6. *Creates Protective Environment.* The supervisor creates a protective environment for the trainees while they learn to apply their new knowledge or skill.

Systems Thinking: Management at the appropriate level(s) is responsible for creating systems that allow all resources, including human, to operate at peak efficiency. The training system, just like any other system, operates best under certain conditions that must be identified and supported. As the management level most aware of the needs of the trainees, the supervisor must help appropriate levels of management establish policies that will help employees best utilize the training.

7. *Provides Incentive.* The supervisor encourages the trainees to apply learning to the job.

Systems Thinking: Recognizes that human beings are the key to improving business processes and therefore carefully identifies and employs the incentives that drive employees to their most productive behavior.

8. *Coaches/Models.* The supervisor models the performance targeted by the training and coaches the trainees on how to perform at the targeted level.

Systems Thinking: Although this activity flows directly from learning principles, it is supported by the systems thinking principle that supervisor and subordinate should relate to one another as team members whenever feasible and constructive to do so. Perhaps more importantly, at the heart of every activity should be the attitude of continuous improvement, which a supervisor can effectively model even when he or she is unable to coach a subordinate because he or she (the supervisor) does not have the required expertise.

9. *Provides Support Groups.* The supervisor helps create support groups to facilitate transfer.

Systems Thinking: Although this activity directly flows from learning principles, systems thinking supports it by encouraging teaming whenever appropriate. Systems thinking has revealed that there are more opportunities for constructive teaming than has traditionally been recognized.

10. *Has Trainees Train Peers.* The supervisor has trainees develop themselves by training fellow workers.

Systems Thinking: This is an example of one of the opportunities for constructive teaming mentioned in number 9 above.

11. *Documents/Reports on Progress.* The supervisor documents trainees' progress in applying learning to the job and reports to trainees on findings.

Systems Thinking: Requires that processes/performance be measured and monitored first to stabilize them and then to improve them.

Trainee

Systems Thinking. All the activities below (12 through 16) are instances of the general principle that employees should be involved in planning and designing their own work whenever feasible and productive.

12. *Sets Realistic Goals.* The trainee sets realistic goals for himself or herself in a personal action plan (also called a transfer action plan).

13. *Refers to Training Materials.* The trainee refers to training materials to help with recall and understanding.

14. *Uses Buddy System.* The trainee works with a buddy who was chosen during training to help apply what both have learned.

15. *Uses Self-Motivation Techniques.* The trainee uses self-motivation techniques (rewarding himself or herself for successfully applying what has been learned).

16. *Monitors Own Performance.* The trainee monitors his or her own performance to acknowledge success and to improve if there is a problem.

Training Team

Systems Thinking: Systems thinking supports all the activities below (17 through 21) by emphasizing that any activity occurs in a context of interrelated systems—in this case, that formal training is not unconnected to what follows it.

17. *Advises Supervisor.* The team constructively advises supervisors of their subordinates' learning performance, so that supervisors can best help subordinates apply to the job what they learned in training. When possible, emphasizes where supervisors can expect improved performance, so that supervisors' positive expectation will influence the trainees to do well.

18. *Provides Follow-Up Questions/Recognition.* The team members make follow-up phone calls, send follow up questionnaires, and give follow-up recognition to trainees.

19. *Provides Follow Up Readings/Exercises.* The team provides follow-up readings or exercises to aid trainee recall or further development.

20. *Provides Refresher Course.* Training team members provide training that restores any knowledge or skills that have deteriorated since training.

21. *Provides Advanced Training.* The team provides training that extends the knowledge or skills that the trainees developed previously.

Conclusion

Training effectiveness is increased by understanding that training is only one activity among many, all of which are interrelated. Systems thinking tells us that organizations are made up of interrelated processes that must be identified and then stabilized before they and the resulting organizational performance can be continuously and reliably improved. In particular, training effectiveness cannot be maximized without support from executive management, which is responsible for the company system as a whole and the integration of all subsystems.

What is suggested by theory is also supported by experience. The training literature is filled with examples of ineffective training due to lack of executive-level understanding or support. This experience is confirmed by Broad and Newstrom's (1992) research. Their core finding is that training will fail to impact any organization to the degree that it is treated as an isolated process within the system.

References

Broad, M.L., & Newstrom, J.W. (1992). *Transfer of training: Action-packed strategies to ensure high payoff from training investments.* Reading, MA: Addison-Wesley.

Schouborg, G. (1993). *FLEX: A flexible tool for continuously improving your evaluation of training effectiveness.* Amherst, MA: HRD Press.

Gary Schouborg is a partner of Performance Consulting, which improves developmental processes for both individuals and organizations. He received his Ph.D. in philosophical psychology from the University of Texas at Austin and is currently constructing a naturalistic, developmental theory of enlightenment.

HOW TO BE A WORLD-CLASS FACILITATOR OF LEARNING

Robert C. Preziosi and Kitty Preziosi

Abstract: There are many keys to becoming an outstanding facilitator of learning. The focus of this article is to synthesize the most important means of creating and conducting effective learning events. A requisite for any successful training facilitation is love of the job. That cornerstone is covered, followed by the authors' ideas about three key aspects of the facilitation of learning: design, set-up, and delivery.

Introduction

It is possible to build your skills as a world-class facilitator to meet the current universal challenge to improve everyone's knowledge and skills. As skills build, so do credibility and reputation. Learners will seek you out and look forward to sessions with you. In this article we share some key building blocks from our experience of training and consulting with learners at all levels of business and government agencies around the world.

Love Your Job

To be really effective and ultimately successful in a job—no matter what it is—a real love for the work is a strong propeller. To be an educator of adults, you must love what you are doing. The nature of our work is to help others be successful. If we do not love the work, our help and facilitation will not seem sincere and the outcomes will not be fruitful for the learners. The love for your work must be clearly telegraphed in everything you do, inside and outside of the classroom. "Love Your Job" is thus the cornerstone for anyone wanting to be a superior facilitator of learning.

Loving your job, however, is just the jumping-off point. In order to be an effective facilitator, you must pay careful attention to three aspects of training design: design, set-up, and delivery, all of which are covered in the following sections.

Design

First, you must *be aware of learners' motivations and needs.* People come to a learning situation for a variety of reasons. Some come because their boss directs them, some come because of their own achievement orientation, and others come for a host of other reasons. We as facilitators of learning must find out *why* they are there and what they expect to gain. We must be careful not to project our own needs on the learning population, but must focus on what our learners require from us and from the learning environment to be successful.

Second, *be aware of learning styles.* We want, of course, to teach in a way that is most comfortable for us. However, the focus should be on the learners and their preferences. Some people learn best when they hear (auditory learners), some when they see (visual learners), and some when they do (active learners). As a matter of fact, most adults probably learn better when they see *and* do. Several learning style instruments are available for determining learners' styles, including the Learning Style Inventory (Kolb, 1985), which identifies four learning styles.

Third, *consider the learners' stages of life development.* All of us are probably familiar with the stages of human development that we have studied or heard about. In her popular book, *New Passages,* Gail Shechy (1995) reminded us again that adults go through developmental stages also. Sheehy also said that adults have different needs at different stages. We as trainers have to be sensitive to developmental stages. Another resource for understanding developmental stages and their impact on adult teaching and learning processes is Keegan (1982). Become a student of your own and your participants' developmental needs. Ask the learners to complete a questionnaire prior to your session so you can discover their needs.

Fourth, *consider differences in values.* Design for differences. People have different value systems, the result being that they frame educational experiences in different ways. Be familiar with and comfortable with this process, whether it is conceptual or abstract, hands-on or theoretical. Help learners understand their own values with regard to the topic. Drive home the point that there often is more than one way to approach and/or analyze any situation and the people involved. There may be more than one valid perspective. We as facilitators also have to be comfortable with multiple value systems.

Fifth, *use learners' past experiences.* When you introduce a new concept, a new behavior, or a new skill, anchor it to something learners know. This gives the learners a frame of reference, without which it will take much longer for them to learn. The key is to identify a generic experience or bit of knowledge that learners can relate to their own past experiences. These may not always touch every learner, so provide other experiences, examples, or pieces of knowledge to help those who cannot relate to the first one. Whatever program you are doing, whatever kind of session, the content and material must be tied to past experiences. Adult learners must have a starting place.

Sixth, *plan meaningful activities.* As we clearly know, the adult learner must be *engaged* in order to learn. The activities used in the learning event must be relevant for the audience. Each audience has different characteristics. For example, a group of thirty-year-olds has a different perspective from a group of twenty-year-olds. And a group of executives has a different context than a group of supervisors or a group of front-line employees. Learners must be able to relate to and learn from our examples and activities.

Seventh, *make training immediately applicable.* Make sure that whatever you teach can be integrated into learners' jobs or into their lives. Show how learners can immediately use what is being presented. "Immediate" can mean different things, but we interpret it to mean that learners will be able to *use* a concept, a skill, or a behavior as soon as the session ends. *Immediate applicability* creates added value and makes your participants more receptive. For example, if you are training learners to use a new software package, its use in the workplace should be imminent. Otherwise, the new knowledge or skill may be forgotten and the training will have to be repeated.

When learners leave the training room, they must take something that they are capable of integrating into their activities. It is a mistake to assume that their active participation in the learning event means that they will use the learning on the job as intended. How can you tell? You developed, you designed, you delivered, but how do you know that learners are able to integrate the learning afterward? You can help ensure after-class application by asking probing questions of the participants, asking them how they will use the knowledge gained. You can use "applied learning forms," a one-page tool that requires learners to commit to actions they will take after they leave the learning session. (An example is shown in Figure 1.) When learners return for another learning event, it is very important for them to discuss how they integrated their previous learning into their work or into their personal lives.

Last, *take advantage of visual learning.* People can learn a lot from what they see, even if they are not visual learners, so visuals are very important. We know that adults remember best what they see or hear first and what they have seen or heard most recently. Thus, the material presented in the middle of your program is less likely to be remembered. At the mid-point we as trainers should be more involved with the participants and have them become more involved with each other. The more visuals—overhead projection, flip charts, etc.—during the training, the better chance of participants retaining the content.

SET-UP

A Comfortable Learning Environment. Some learning experts have suggested that unless the environment is comfortable, people will not learn anything. We strongly agree. It can be relatively easy to create a comfortable physical

Reinforced Learning

The most valuable things I was reminded of during today's class session were:

A.

B.

C.

New Learning

The most valuable new concept(s), techniques(s) or strategy(ies) that I learned about during today's class session were:

A.

B.

C.

Applied Learning

I will apply one new concept, technique, or strategy at work to add value in the following way:

Learning Need

Something I would like to learn more about after today's class session that would add more value at work is:

Learning Plan (What, from Whom, Where, When)

I will learn more about the above by:

A.

B.

C.

Figure 1. Sample Applied Learning Form

environment; however, trainers do not always do the things necessary to ensure that participants are comfortable. For example, we have known for at least twenty-five years that incandescent lighting is better in a classroom or training room than fluorescent lighting. However, to conserve energy we more frequently use fluorescent lighting. We sometimes find that the seating is not appropriate. The chairs may be so uncomfortable that no one can sit in them for more than five or ten minutes. Often there are barriers that we cannot overcome because our client organization has limits. But we must do everything that we can to make the setting physically comfortable for our participants.

A High-Impact Beginning. The first few minutes of interaction set the tone for the entire session. A high-impact start includes a touch of humor, some eye-opening data, a brief and focused statement of the expected outcome(s), complete attention to each person's introduction, use of everyone's name, a twenty-second (or less) answer to any question, positive eye contact, and a friendly but firm interactive style (Preziosi, 1994). If an icebreaker is used, it should tie in directly to the expected outcome(s) of the session (Preziosi, 1999). Avoid devaluing the session by apologizing or making excuses for the unimportant things.

Energy and Interaction. Keep yourself energized physically, mentally, and emotionally. Your participants will likely follow your lead and feel more energized themselves. Solid interaction is the result of your warm, friendly interactive style from the first contact with your participants. Even a welcoming statement on the overhead or flip chart generates interactivity. Make it easy for participants to interact by using nametags.

Starting on time is energizing because your participants' energy is rising toward the published start time, and that energy will only dissipate when it is not put to use.

A very important, but often overlooked, concern is the refreshments or meals that are provided. Foods that keep energy high in the morning are coffees, teas, juices, and fruit, not bagels, muffins, or doughnuts! At the noon hour provide chicken, salads, vegetables, and clear soups. Fish is great, but some do not care for it. Be sure to avoid turkey, beef, heavy starch, and anything fried. If you provide dessert or snacks, fruit or a small amount of something made of chocolate works well.

Transfer of Learning. What good is the time spent with you in the training if the learning is not used later? There is tremendous opportunity to impact the business through your training programs if you work hard to ensure transfer of learning.

Your first task is to meet with your learners' supervisors to discuss their expectations of the learning and to set forth some tasks for them. These would include such things as a supervisor-learner pre-training conference to reinforce the value of the training program and a supervisor-learner post-training conference to discuss what the participants learned and how it will be applied on the job. You would also discuss with the supervisor ways to incorporate the learning applications from the training into the performance management and appraisal processes.

Throughout the training, ask learners how they will apply their learning. Include small-group discussions with reporting out as part of your learning design. And, of course, use applied learning forms.

Job aids and other learning tools can be valuable for learning transfer. Online job aids can also be tremendously useful. For example, use an e-mail attachment to send a brainstormed list or other products from a learning session to an entire training group. You could also provide your participants with audiotapes of the session or of other relevant information.

Fun. Everyone likes to have fun. Games provide a wonderful opportunity. You can create greater learning success by integrating games into your session (Salopek, 1999; Sugar, 1998). They are also energizing. However, before using games, be sure your corporate culture is accepting of the idea.

People also enjoy music. You can use it in a variety of ways. One of the most popular is using classical music for "concert (content) review." We have also found it useful for "concert preview." Energizing music is useful when participants are returning from a break. You can also find great music to inject into specific training content. For example, one of the authors used segments of "The Best" by Tina Turner, "One Moment in Time" by Whitney Houston, and "Wind Beneath My Wings" by Bette Midler during a program on self-esteem for nurses.*

Finally, there are props and toys. Here you can be very creative. One of the authors currently uses small stuffed animals in discussion of certain leadership practices. Another idea is to use a full-size plastic bowling pin to emphasize the importance of hitting targets during a class on performance management. Visit stores that sell toys and/or party supplies. Wander around the store, letting your mind replay your instructional design as you look at things and ask yourself: "How can I use this to make or reinforce a learning point?"

---

*Always be aware of copyright issues when using music and obtain permission prior to your session if necessary.

DELIVERY

Meet Expectations—Theirs and Yours. Any time a trainer introduces a new program, it is essential to establish learning expectations. What do you want your learners to do? Do you want them to be involved a great deal in the classroom activities, or do you want them merely to sit quietly and listen to you? In ninety-nine cases out of one hundred, passive yet attentive listening will not suffice for adult learners. It is necessary for the participants to be involved in the learning experience. We want participants to have a positive frame of mind—to be told that this will be a positive learning opportunity for them. In contrast, we would never tell them: "This is going to be difficult," "It's a tough course," "It'll be a tough three days," or anything like that. We want to begin on a positive, upbeat note. This increases the probability of successful learning outcomes.

Ask the group what they expect. What do they want you to do? Do they want you to challenge their ideas? Do they want you to guide discussions very specifically? Do they want you to provide specific learning aids or job aids, or do they expect you to just talk and allow them to listen? Find out early what they think and what they want you to do. That will help you integrate their perspective with your perspective. It will help you decide who needs more independence as a learner and who requires more guidance and direction.

"Hands-On" Learning. In everything you say and do, emphasize that learning application is hands-on. Without that strategy, the learning outcomes may be construed as knowledge for knowledge's sake, and the participants may feel no real responsibility for doing something with what's learned. The participants must know it's going to be "hands-on" learning and that they are expected to do something differently as a result of the learning event. Hands on is often thought to be physical only. But it can be "hearts on" (dealing with affect or attitude) or "heads on" (dealing with cognitive elements).

Nudge Your Learners. We know from learning masters such as Malcolm Knowles (Knowles, Holton, & Swanson, 1998) that adults are self-directed, so approach adult education as a self-directed process. Of course, our experience has shown that not all adults are self-directed learners, even though we may want them to be. Do what you can to nudge adults along, to help adults develop, to help them move from one developmental stage to the next so that they are indeed self-directed learners. After they become self-directed, it is much easier to teach and train them, so determine each person's perspective and work from there.

Create a Positive Environment. Create a supportive environment. People want a trainer who welcomes them, someone who is there with a smile, someone who is pleasant to talk to, who enjoys talking with them. People don't want trainers who frown because they've had an unpleasant experience just before arriving. It is important that you be as positive as you possibly can.

Deliver to and for the Audience. Know what the benefits of the learning are for every person. The adult learner says: "Okay, here I am. What am I going to get out of this? Will I receive a promotion? Will I be in consideration for a promotion? Will I get a raise? Will I become better able to compete in the marketplace? What will I get out of this?" Maybe the answer is as simple as personal satisfaction for completing a learning event. Frame for people what they are going to get out of the training. Some organizations provide financial incentives for those who complete certain training programs. That is wonderful motivation, but it is not available to everyone, so you will have to find other ways. Find other options for helping each person to define what the benefits of a particular program are going to be for him or her. Without knowledge and acceptance of those benefits, a learner attains less valuable outcomes.

Use Summaries. As leaders of the adult learning process, summarize the learning for the participants often. Pull things together for them. This helps to reinforce the learning and enhances the chance that it will be retained. You must have complete and total grasp of the material in order to summarize it well. Summarize as often as possible—the key points, the behavioral parts, the conceptual parts, everything. Learners consistently report that this improves closure and application.

Address Requirements While in the classroom, individuals have professional needs, personal needs, or a combination of the two, so the material or the content that you are addressing must be related to both. Understandably, it is not always possible to build a relationship of content to current needs for every person publicly in the classroom. You may have to spend time individually with the learner, which can be as important as the public process with the entire group. Working with each individual is essential; it is fundamental. Tying the material in to individual needs adds value to the process.

Use Learners as a Resource. Use the experience of the learners as a resource. Involve them in discussions. Ask them to exchange experiences. Emphasize how important their experiences are to what they have learned, what they are learning, what they will learn. This will give the learning episode much greater impact. Remember, each of us carries around an invisible sign that states, "I am important. Listen to me. Let me tell you about my experiences." New trainers often make the mistake of believing that they must do all the talking. The irony is that the best adult learning environment involves the learners as active contributors to the process. This enhances participants' self-esteem and validates the utility of these experiences.

Control the Classroom. Create and maintain a positive learning environment in the classroom. Control is a part of it. "Control" is not always a negative word. You have to have control. You need to know what is going on in your classrooms. Give some direction, even though you are dealing with many adults who may be totally self-directed. Control the situation so that they form peer learning networks. Maintain control so that you can nudge them along when they need to be nudged along.

Maintain Participants' Self-Esteem. Always protect minority opinions— the opinions that are not shared by many people in the classroom. When you have discussions in class and ask for opinions, many people will support one perspective, and a small group will not. It would be very easy to say: "Okay, it's all right. There can be disagreement." In reality, that small group that is not aligned with the larger group may feel a drop in self-esteem, although it may not be apparent. Therefore, it is very important to ensure that everyone's self-esteem is maintained. Protect the minority opinion by protecting their perspective, because nothing is more important in your training room than self-esteem. If training or education is going to be successful, then trainers must do everything in their power to maintain or enhance self-esteem of participants. Esteemed learners are more successful.

Be a Role Model. Be a model of everything that adult learning and organizational training stand for. For example, if you are leading a discussion about the importance of participation and respect for each individual, be a model in that process. Allow for complete and total respect for each of the individuals who is present. Whether the issue is respect or something else, encourage learners to reflect critically on their attitudes, beliefs, and/or behaviors. This will help them confirm or realize a need for change. By being a model, you can challenge individual attitudes, beliefs, and behaviors. People *must* come to grips with what they see and what they hear, with what they understand and with what they learn. And the best vehicle for that challenge is the trainer's behavior. So challenge learners through your thought patterns and your behavior.

Also, model the values and performance that your organizational culture supports. For example, if timeliness is an organizational value, then start and end all sessions on time.

Summary

There are many opinions about what can make the difference in design, set-up, and delivery of a learning event. If you have a love for your job as a facilitator of learning, you can adopt these tips to help your learners achieve relevant, vibrant, long-lasting learning.

References

Kegan, R. (1982). *The evolving self.* Cambridge, MA: Harvard University Press.

Knowles, M., Holton, E., & Swanson, R. (1998). *The definitive classic on adult education and training.* Houston, TX: Gulf.

Kolb, D.A. (1985). *Learning style inventory.* Boston, MA: McBer.

Preziosi, R. (1994). *Tens ways to create a motivating learning environment.* APICS Proceedings. Falls Church, VA: American Production and Inventory Control Society.

Preziosi, R. (1999). Icebreakers. *Info-line.* Alexandria, VA: American Society for Training and Development.

Salopek, J. (1999, February). Stop playing games. *Training & Development,* pp. 26-30.

Sheehy, G. (1995). *New passages: Mapping your life across time.* New York: Random House.

Sugar, S. (1998). *Games that teach.* San Francisco, CA: Jossey-Bass/Pfeiffer.

Robert C. Preziosi, D.P.A., is a professor of management at the Huizenga Graduate School of Business and Entrepreneurship at Nova Southeastern University in Fort Lauderdale, Florida. In 1997 he received the school's first Excellence in Teaching Award. He is also president of Preziosi Partners, Inc., a consulting firm. He has worked as a human resources director, a line manager, and a leadership-training administrator. As a trainer, his areas of interest include leadership, adult learning, and all aspects of management and executive development. In 1984 he was given the Outstanding Contribution to HRD award by ASTD, and in 1996 he received his second ASTD Torch Award. He is a regular contributor to the Annuals.

Kitty Preziosi is a corporate catalyst at Preziosi Partners, Inc., in Fort Lauderdale, Florida. She has over twenty years' experience as executive in charge or senior consultant of training and organization development for major corporations such as Visa International, The Coca-Cola Company, ABB Combustion Engineering, New South, and United Technologies. Her focus areas are performance management, strategic change implementation, management development, and sales training. She has been a featured speaker at local, regional, and international ASTD conferences.

CREATIVELY DEBRIEFING GROUP ACTIVITIES

Andy Beaulieu

Abstract: As trainers and facilitators, we put great effort
and care into selecting or even developing appropriate and engaging learning activities for our groups.
Yet few facilitators put much thought at all into the
process of debriefing. And the published, structured
activities, now widely available in sources such as this
one, offer little support; they may prescribe the main
activity itself in great detail, but often do little more
than list some recommended debriefing questions.
The selection of a debriefing process is rarely addressed. As most facilitators have come to realize, the
quality of the debriefing can make or break the value
of the activity for the participants. This discussion
identifies the challenges inherent in the debriefing
process and the principles behind creative, capable
debriefing. Finally, a sample debriefing process called
"Talk Show Host" is included, as both an example of
creative debriefing and to provide one process that
can be used immediately in many situations.

$\mathbf{P}$icture this perhaps all-too-familiar scene:

> A group has just completed a very participative and engaging experiential learning activity when the facilitator snaps back into role: "Okay, now everyone take your seats. All right, let's talk about what just happened. Who can tell me what they observed? C'mon, who will start?"

> Which of the following describes what will happen next:

1. All participants start talking at once, barely able to contain their thoughts and feelings.

2. One participant starts the discussion, the rest chiming in and building off one another's comments.

3. All participants stare down at the table hoping not to be called on, because no matter how powerful the activity no one likes to sit and talk in a group.

If you picked "3," you are aware of the challenges of debriefing group activities. Even the most relevant and revealing activity can fall prey to an uninspired debriefing process. Sitting a group down after such an activity and throwing out such questions as "What did we see happen?" and "What might that tell us about our interaction back on the job?" can instantly bring the energy and participation level of the group down to zero.

WHAT IS DEBRIEFING?

In general, debriefing occurs right after the experiential learning activity itself and is intended to help participants identify what happened and why and then to apply those same findings to their organizations. To accomplish this diagnosis, facilitators often pose questions much like the following:

1. What happened during the activity?

2. Why did it happen?

3. Does anything like that ever happen at work?

4. Why does it happen?

5. What might you do differently to improve the work situation?

This sequence of questions leads the participants down a path from recall and diagnosis to application and intervention. A successful debriefing can help participants apply learnings from even a simple activity to their work lives. Most trainers, facilitators, and educators will readily admit that debriefing is critical to the success of the experiential learning activity. Yet few recognize the challenges inherent in debriefing; even fewer know how to overcome these challenges.

DEBRIEFING IS CHALLENGING

Although behavior during a group activity may be spontaneous, processing that experience is a different and generally more demanding skill. Specifically, debriefing is difficult because it forces individuals:

- To offer comments and insights without much preparation;

- To follow a very logical, structured process known only to the facilitator;

- To speak in public;

- To conduct often complex behavioral analysis;

- To discuss a situation they experienced but did not objectively observe; and

- To talk openly about the behavior and motives of others during the activity.

Given these challenges, it becomes clear that facilitators must put as much care into their debriefing process as they do into selecting (or developing) the learning activity itself. An appropriate debriefing process will make it easy for all participants to engage in the process and produce the desired learning outcomes.

PRINCIPLES OF CREATIVE DEBRIEFING

Overcoming the challenges listed above requires a bit of creativity and some planning. Debriefing processes that engage the audience can be developed based on the following five principles:

1. Reveal the entire set of debriefing questions at the outset to allow participants to see the debriefing road map and prepare.

2. Allow participants to respond to the debriefing questions individually before volunteering their information to the group.

3. Use processing at the pair and small subgroup level to increase the accountability and involvement by each participant.

4. Use a game-like format to extend the energy and playfulness of the original learning activity through to the debriefing.

5. Stage the debriefing in a way that allows participants to answer to one another rather than to the facilitator.

Clearly, not all of these principles need be applied in every situation. But finding ways to incorporate as many of them as possible increases the chances of an engaging, successful debriefing process.

A CREATIVE DEBRIEFING PROCESS

Presented on the next pages is a creative debriefing technique called "Talk Show Host." The process works well because it allows participants to prepare for the debriefing, employs a fun approach, and maintains focus on the participants rather than on the facilitator. In fact, it manages to apply all five of the principles outlined above.

TALK SHOW HOST: DEBRIEFING EXPERIENTIAL ACTIVITIES

Goal

- To facilitate the debriefing of any group experiential activity by increasing participant involvement and accountability, maintaining a high level of energy, and allowing participants time to prepare their responses.

Group Size

This process is designed to be used after an experiential activity involving two or three subgroups of virtually any size.

Time Required

Forty minutes to prepare and close, plus about fifteen minutes per subgroup.

Materials

- None

Physical Setting

Participants should be seated together with those from their experiential activity subgroup.

Preparation

Write the debriefing questions on a board or flip chart for all to see.

Process

1. Instruct participants that you would like to give them a chance to review the activity just completed and extract any learnings. Explain that the way you would like to do this is to have each group be interviewed by a member of one of the other groups. Say that the interviewer will adopt the personae of a well-known talk show host to present the debriefing questions shown on the flip chart and to challenge them to expand their thinking. When the interviewer is satisfied with all of their answers, they must try to guess which real-life talk show host was being impersonated. Then the questioning will switch to the next team. (Five minutes.)

2. Review the debriefing questions you have developed and posted. Tell the teams they will have twenty minutes to prepare their answers to the debriefing questions, as well as to select one of their group members to serve as an interviewer. The interviewer should contribute to the team's preparation, but at the same time select a talk show host persona to adopt and prepare to interview another team. Tell the interviewers that they may employ different tactics, but that they should all dig beyond the first answers they receive to "get the scoop." (Five minutes.)

3. Ask whether there are any questions about the debriefing questions or the process to be followed. Begin the twenty-minute preparation period. (Twenty minutes.)

4. After preparations are complete, select one team to be interviewed first and select the interviewer. Position the interviewer in a chair very close to and facing the team to be interviewed. Provide the time limit, if any, and then let the interviewer conduct the debriefing. Interject only to provide any time warnings. (Fifteen minutes.)

5. At the end of the first team's debriefing, ask the team what talk show host was being impersonated. Ask what makes the team think this. Invite the interviewer to confirm or rebut the guess. Offer applause if the environment is conducive. (Two minutes.)

6. Repeat Steps 4 and 5 for each additional team and interviewer. With three teams, be careful not to end up with the last team being interviewed by its own member. (Fifteen minutes per additional team.)

7. After all teams are finished, you may want to facilitate a summary of at least the action items across all teams. Like any form of training or facilitation, experiential exercises do little good if no actions are taken or changes are made as a result. (Ten minutes.)

Variation

■ In order to increase the depth of the questioning, use interviewer pairs rather than individuals. While one person plays the "lead" and poses the initial questions, both interviewers conceive and pose probing/follow-on questions. This will increase the time of the debriefing somewhat.

References

Beaulieu, A., & Pernick, R. (1999). Samoan circle: A large group dialogue process. In M. Silberman (Ed.), *The 1999 team and organization development sourcebook.* New York: McGraw-Hill.

Lucker, J.L., & Nadler, R.S. (1997). *Processing the experience: Strategies to enhance and generalize learning.* Dubuque, IA: Kendall/Hunt.

Andy Beaulieu is an organization effectiveness consultant based in Bethesda, Maryland, who has consulted to clients such as Fidelity Investments, NASDAQ, American Airlines, British Petroleum, Veterans Administration Hospitals, SAFE-LITE AutoGlass, World Bank, and Showtime Networks. This submission is drawn from his new book, Never Ask a Group a Question: 25 Creative Ways to Debrief a Group Activity.

CUSTOMIZED PROBLEM-SOLVING AND DECISION-MAKING ACTIVITIES

Donald T. Simpson

Abstract: Customized training materials spark interest and participation and enhance credibility. Learners are more apt to connect with familiar content and accept activities they perceive as relevant and credible, so are more likely to try out concepts back on the job. Customization must be field-specific, but not real-life. Participants must be able to disengage from the content when the activity is over and reflect on what was learned. Your purpose is to help participants learn process skills, not just solve one problem. This article describes a method for customizing a popular activity for group problem solving and decision making.

INTRODUCTION

Customized, content-relevant training materials spark interest and foster participation. Learners view the material and the activity as relevant to their work. Taking the time to customize your learning materials tells participants that you care about practical application. However, many trainers feel they do not have the design skills or the time to customize their materials. This article presents an approach to customizing materials that can be time-efficient, effective, and fun.

WHEN TO CONSIDER CUSTOMIZING

Homogeneous groups offer the best opportunity for customizing for maximum participation and application. Designing materials and activities that use language and examples built from the participants' work culture builds a bridge of rapport between trainer and learner. The material comes alive and becomes relevant, and there is instant face validity. Participants are more likely to try out new skills when motivated by the idea of learning something they perceive they can apply back on the job.

Sometimes customizing is inappropriate and difficult. For example, open-enrollment training sessions or public workshops present a challenge. When participants represent widely diverse constituencies (say, financial institutions, manufacturing, office operations, children's homes, and local government), it can be difficult to find a common denominator. Under these circumstances, trainers save time and effort by using a tested, reliable, generic activity.

WHAT TO CUSTOMIZE

If you want to teach participants a problem-solving technique, you want them to focus on the process, not the particulars. Although occasionally a class can learn the underlying process by addressing a real-life problem, generally real-life issues interfere with global learning. Real-life issues raise the emotional ante. Participants become too involved in the content. They become more interested in addressing the particular issue than in learning how to address such issues in general.

Customizing must reflect the participants' job lives, but still be apart from the job. After the activity, participants drop back from the content and examine their process objectively. That way, they can examine their strengths, identify areas for improvement, and learn new skills.

Customized training that directly reflects the organization's environment results in high credibility. However, if you are unfamiliar with your participants' environment, this kind of customizing can be difficult. Credibility can actually be reduced if customization is not done well. For example, the misuse of jargon, an incorrect technical term, or an unintentional reference to an inappropriate past event may actually reduce credibility. Participants will see the exercise as a poor attempt by an outsider to mirror their world.

It is thus easier to customize with content from the participants' *field* rather than from a specific work environment. This type of customization still supports credibility and interest, yet distances the activity enough from real-life experience for participants to remain objective about their process. And it's a lot easier to design and prepare.

HOW TO CUSTOMIZE A PROBLEM-SOLVING ACTIVITY

In this particular case, your training objective is to have participants examine their information-sharing and decision-making processes in work teams. In order to reach this objective, you've chosen a popular problem-solving/decision-making activity, in which members of a small group have different elements of information they must share and process to solve the problem or make the decision. The following steps can be taken for customizing:

- Analyze the audience;
- Select a topic;
- Develop decision criteria;
- Describe choices;
- Prepare the scenario;
- Prepare participant materials; and
- Pilot the activity.

Analyze the Audience

Identify participants' job functions. The more you know about them, the better you can meet their needs through customizing. Ask your client contact well in advance of the class for a roster that includes names, job titles, and departments of participants.

> *Example:* You are preparing a class in team problem solving and decision making for a local law enforcement agency. The class will consist of deputies and other employees from the sheriff's office. About half are from the road patrol, and half are divided among court protection, jailers, and administrative staff.

Select a Topic

Consider a topic that requires the team to make a choice from several clearly defined alternatives. Tailor the subject matter to the team's work. The task may be a purchase decision, a hiring decision, a budget decision, or a new product or service decision. The topic and the decision should reflect the team's work environment, but not be from real life. If you have a class of business managers, you'll most likely select an accounting or business decision, such as where to locate a new plant, which plant to close down, or what new product to develop. For community agency administrators, you might select a service or budget decision, such as what services to introduce or cut back or where to open a new outreach center.

> *Example:* For the sheriff's office, you select a purchase decision involving a hand-held laser speed gun. This topic is field-specific, appealing very directly to half the class—deputies in the road patrol. The other half of the class can relate to the topic, even if indirectly.

Develop Decision Criteria

All decisions are made against some criteria, whether implicit or explicit. One of your objectives is to make participants more aware of their decision criteria. You will select clear criteria. The group uses the criteria you provide to make the decision. The team, through sharing and discussing available information, must discern whether an option meets the criteria.

Example: You choose six criteria:

- Range > 750 yards
- Cost < $1500
- Instant-on
- Zero EMF
- Immediately available
- Mid-range accuracy ± 3 mi/hr

Describe Choices

Create four to seven options from which the team must select one that meets all the decision criteria. Describe options such that only one option meets all the necessary criteria. Depending on your learning objectives, you may include some ambiguous elements for the team to resolve. It is useful to make a grid of the criteria and the options, such as the one in Figure 1. The solution grid describes the criteria and shows which choices meet which criteria. Notice that no special knowledge of law enforcement, electronics, or departmental procedures is needed to solve the problem. You do not show participants the solution grid until the exercise is over.

Model⁣ Requirement	HotShot 1200	Zapper Trooper	White Lightning	ZOT 55-Alive	X-File 6640
Range > 750 yards	10–900 yds	10–800 yds	10–600 yds	10–850 yds	10–800 yds
Cost < $1500	$1400	$1250	$1050	$1700	$1400
Instant-On	Yes	Yes	Yes	Yes	No
Zero EMF	Yes	Yes	Yes	Yes	Yes
Immediately Available	Yes	6 mo	Yes	Yes	Yes
Mid-Range Accuracy ±3 mi/hr	±3 mi/hr	±2 mi/hr	±3 mi/hr	±3 mi/hr	±3 mi/hr

▢ Eliminates this option

Figure 1. Sample Solution Grid (Not Provided to Participants)

A specification sheet describes the options for participants. Figure 2 is an example of a specification sheet developed for this session.

Example: You develop specifications for five fictitious models in contention among the sheriff's office team. All but one model fails to meet a criterion. You decide to include some ambiguous elements that the team must discuss, for example, is "ship in one week" the same as "immediately available"? Is "five seconds acquisition time" the same as "instant-on"?

Laser Hand-Held Speed Measuring Devices Product Specifications

HotShot 1200

Source: HotShot Electronics, Inc., Chicago

Weight: 4 lbs, 6 oz

Range: 10–900 yards

Accuracy at Mid-Range: 3 mi/hr

EMF Emissions: Zero

Special Features/Information: Fog/clear settings. Instant activation. Safety lens. Ship in one week.

Cost: $1,400

Zapper Trooper Model

Source: Minnesota Law Enforcement Equipment Company, St. Paul

Weight: 4 lbs

Range: 10–800 yards

Accuracy at Mid-Range: 2 mi/hr

EMF Emissions: Zero

Special Features/Information: Instant activation. Safety lens. Will be available in about six months.

Cost: $1,250

White Lightning

Source: White Electronics, New York City

Weight: 4 lbs, 8 oz

Range: 10–600 yards

Accuracy at Mid-Range: 3 mi/hr

EMF Emissions: Zero

Special Features/Information: Instant activation. Immediately available.

Cost: $1,050

ZOT Model 55-Alive

Source: Zebra Optical Technologies, Inc., Los Angeles

Weight: 4 lbs, 10 oz

Range: 10–850 yards

Accuracy at Mid-Range: 3 mi/hr

EMF Emissions: Zero

Special Features/Information: Fog/clear settings. Instant activation. Safety lens. Ship in one week.

Cost: $1,700

X-File Model 5640

Source: Prison Industries, Joliet, Illinois

Weight: 4 lbs, 3 oz

Range: 10–800 yards

Accuracy at Mid-Range: 3 mi/hr

EMF Emissions: Zero

Special Features/Information: Fog/clear and psychic settings. Immediately available. 3 seconds acquisition time.

Cost: $1,400

Figure 2. Sample Specification Sheet (Given to All Participants)

Prepare the Scenario

Prepare a plausible scenario for the decision worksheet, keeping your audience in mind.

Example: You prepare the decision worksheets for the sheriff's office team. All worksheets contain identical language about the laser speed detector purchase and the specific task of the team. Each decision worksheet, however, contains information about purchase criteria not found on other worksheets. Participants must share information to solve the problem and make the decision. The information in Figure 3 is identical—except for the last paragraph of each sheet. Do not call this to the attention of the participants—that's for them to figure out.

Laser Speed Detector Purchase Decision

You are a Police Department team chartered to determine the best laser hand-held speed detection device for use by the road patrols. Your team has narrowed the decision to five promising models. These are listed on the Specifications Sheet.

The laser gun is especially useful for speed detection in clear weather. It's laser beam is more difficult to detect than traditional radar. Also, the laser device can employ an instant-on. By the time a speeding motorist detects the beam, it's too late. The instant-on feature is an especially desirable advantage of this device.

An absolute requirement by the Department is that the laser device have zero EMF emmissions. This requirement is for the health and safety of the officers using the device.

The range of the device must be at least 750 yards. Minimum range is not a critical factor. There should be no more than a ±3 miles-per-hour accuracy at mid-range

The cost of the device must not be more than $1500.

The device must be immediately available in anticipation of the busy motoring season just ahead.

The cost of the device must not be more than $1500. It must be immediately available in anticipation of the busy motoring season just ahead.

**Figure 3. Sample Decision Worksheet
(Separate Sheets for Each Participant)**

Prepare Participant Materials

Prepare your handouts to complement the activity. Proofread everything to ensure clarity for your participants. After the activity, provide participants with the opportunity to reflect on what happened and their own behaviors. A reaction sheet like the one in Figure 4 helps bring the activity to a close and prepares participants for processing the experience. Having participants reflect individually on their roles in the decision meeting refocuses them from the content to the process.

Instructions: As an individual, please answer the following questions. You'll have the opportunity to share your feelings and suggestions with the rest of your team later.

1. How confident are you that the team solution is correct?

1	2	3	4	5
Not Confident			Very Confident	

2. What did you do that helped the team achieve its goal?

3. What did you do that did not help, and may even have hindered, the team?

4. What did you learn about yourself and the way you interact with others on the team?

5. What emotions did you feel during this activity?

6. List below any personal feedback you would like to provide (one-to-one):

To: _____

To: _____

Figure 4.   Sample Reaction Sheet

Pilot the Activity

Pilot the activity and make adjustments, if needed. At a minimum, explain the activity to someone in the field or in the client organization. Have that person become your content expert and request comments on the material. Are the criteria reasonable? If you have used jargon, is it appropriate? Are the scenarios credible?

Coaching Option

If you are customizing the activity for a large group, you might use subgroups for the team activity. In this case, you may want to use coaches from the organization (perhaps people who have taken the course previously) to provide feedback during processing. Using organizational coaches enhances credibility, lets each subgroup have its own mentor, and provides a great developmental experience for the coaches.

Brief the coaches well before the session, explaining the mechanics of the activity and their role. Provide them with a format to use in providing feedback or processing the discussion. You may wish to develop a coach's briefing sheet like the one in Figure 5.

SUMMARY

Customization of your training materials provides content-relevant learning activities and enhances the credibility of your training. Participants more readily accept activities they perceive as relevant and credible. They are more likely to try out the concepts in class *and* back on the job. Your customized activities must be straightforward, clear, and field-specific, but not real-life. Participants must be able to disengage from the content when the activity is over and re-engage on a process level. Keep in mind your purpose—for the participants to learn process skills, not to solve just one problem.

Donald T. Simpson, Ed.D., is a management and organization development consultant based in Rochester, New York. He has over twenty-five years' experience in industry, health care, community services, and government. He is especially active in total quality deployment and training. He has master's degrees in mechanical engineering and adult learning and holds a doctorate in human and organization development from the Fielding Institute. His published work appears in many recognized handbooks and journals.

As you facilitate the feedback session, remember that you are not delivering a report card. Rather, you are facilitating the session. Your aim is to elicit participation from the team members, not provide your own critique. Here's a suggested agenda:

1. Review the process (agenda) with the group. Select a scribe and a timekeeper.

2. Ask the team leader the following questions:

   - How do you feel about the meeting?

   - What went well? What would you do differently?

   - Before we solicit feedback from the group, on what behaviors would you like some specific feedback?

   Have the scribe list the responses on a flip chart.

3. Ask the group:

   - What went well for you as team members?

   - What specific suggestions would you like to offer?

   Have the recorder list the responses on a flip chart. During this part of the session, only acknowledge the group's observations; do not respond to what is said.

4. Ask questions to elicit useful comments from the group. Avoid overkill. Try to sense when there is enough feedback. Throughout the session:

   - Keep it specific.

   - Keep it timely.

   - Keep it task-related.

5. You may add observations of your own after the group provides its feedback. Don't repeat a previous observation.

6. Ask the team leader:

   - Would you like to comment on any of the feedback?

   The leader may identify feedback on which he or she will take action or may just say "Thank you" to the group. Avoid putting the team leader on the spot or creating a situation in which he or she feels defensive. The leader does not owe the group a response.

7. Thank the team members for their objective comments and their spirit of helpfulness. Thank the leader for his or her willingness to accept feedback. Thank the timekeeper and scribe. Take down the flip charts and give them to the leader.

Figure 5. Sample Coach's Briefing Sheet

CREATING
RELATIONSHIP AND AGREEMENT:
"YOU GET WHAT YOU ASK FOR"

Neil J. Simon

Abstract: Often executives find themselves angry, disappointed, and/or dismayed over team results. They have difficulty understanding why teams do not produce what has been requested of them. Often the teams miss the mark, and quality of product, timeliness of delivery, and inadequate deliverables are issues that often emerge. The executive may play a critical role in the team's lackluster output. This article explores the formative phase of a relationship—what might be called the "agreement" or "commission" between the executive and the team—and what needs to be done to structure the relationship to obtain what is wanted. The article focuses on the art and science of "getting what you ask for" from your teams.

INTRODUCTION

Often an executive has some idea of a desired result but does not necessarily know what effort is needed to accomplish the task. Often when teams do not produce the desired results, the executive doubts their ability to produce. He or she may feel compelled to "micro-manage" or create changes within the team, which too often creates further chaos. The author has developed a self-design method (Simon, 1998a) that helps the executive and team meet each other's professional and personal needs, while at the same time contributing to the overall success of the organization. Several reasons drive organizations to these creative and alternative strategies, such as an increase in competition and the growing complexity of the business environment. To ensure success, it is important to focus and organize the team to achieve the desired results.

CREATING A RELATIONSHIP

Katzenbach and Smith (1993) observed that Hewlett-Packard and Motorola tend to generate effective teams simply by setting forth the right performance challenge to the right set of people. In this context, let's explore the concept of relationship between executives and teams. The first phase in creating relationship, according to the A^2D^4 Self-Design Approach (Simon, 1998a), is to create an agreement between the executive (the sponsor) and the team.

The goal of this first phase is to identify and understand the desired change by developing a common understanding with the sponsor and key stakeholders (other executives and leaders who will be affected by the agreement). The outcome of this phase is to create the focus, scope, project definition, and boundary conditions of the endeavor. A series of tasks must be accomplished. The first task is gaining clarity on what is needed and wanted, including what is—and what is not—negotiable.

Successful initiatives start by building successful relationships between the sponsor and the team. It is in our best interest to create an understanding of the roles and responsibilities of each party.

Roles and Responsibilities

The executive must fulfill certain basic roles and responsibilities to be able to make a valid request of a team. The following is a partial list of those roles and responsibilities:

- Fulfill the legal and fiduciary responsibilities associated with the leadership position;
- Express a vision for the organization, which is explicitly understood;
- Affirm a prioritized set of corporate goals that will help fulfill the vision and provide corporate direction;
- Make decisions in accordance with this vision and its goals and the realities of the market;
- Provide resources to support the organization's progress; and
- Give performance feedback to the organization.

In addition, the sponsor has a critical role in assisting the team to its success. Thus, according to Kern (1997), the sponsor must also:

- Help determine the kind of team required to complete the work under consideration;
- Establish a meaningful performance challenge, while at the same time communicating a high performance standard;
- Promise to provide needed resources and keep those promises;
- Participate in the development of the commission document;
- Create and maintain an atmosphere of trust in the relationship between the team and the organization, including the management structure;
- Establish accountability for the team;
- Provide team development opportunities as needed;
- Provide a link—and not the only link—between the team and its larger environment;
- Offer the team guidance throughout its existence;
- Operate management processes, such as budgets, investment decisions, evaluations, rewards, and compensation, on behalf of the team; and
- Resolve issues and remove obstacles inhibiting the team's performance.

The team also has fundamental roles and responsibilities, including:

- Ensuring that team members fulfill the work contract they have with the organization;
- Understanding the executive vision and ensuring alignment of effort;
- Asking questions to ensure clarity;
- Making decisions in the best interest of the organization;
- Using the organization's resources in the best interest of the organization; and
- Soliciting feedback from executives to ensure being on target.

These roles and responsibilities set the framework of the relationship between the executive and the team. When the executive makes a request (a "commission") of a team, he or she sets up a relationship, that is, creates a promise and commitment. The commission is the output or finished document of the "agree phase" of the self-design process. Initiating this phase launches a relationship process, the *promise and commitment cycle,* which was developed by Amy Kern (1997) and is based on the ActionWorkFlow Loop developed by Flores and Winograd (1997) (see Figure 1). By reviewing the promise and commitment cycle, one can see the subtle aspects of the formation of the relationship and what it takes to create conditions of satisfaction.

Figure 1. The Promise and Commitment Cycle

AN OVERVIEW OF THE PROMISE AND COMMITMENT CYCLE

When the executive or some other individual or team has identified a need or has an idea, he or she prepares to make a request, that is, a "commission," to the team. Alternatively, an individual or team may identify a need within the organization and make an offer to the executive to take some action, possibly requiring the establishment of a team. It is important that the request be well targeted.

The "Promise and Commitment Cycle" shown in Figure 1 illustrates how the process should work. Unfortunately, this is not always what happens. After the request or offer is made, the team will often take the request and run with it. They may think they understand what the executive wants and are eager to meet his or her needs. But there is no clarity of expectations on either side and, in some organizations, the culture may even discourage asking clarifying questions. Assumptions will inevitably be made by both the executive and the team; it is important to be aware of this and to evaluate the risk and to mitigate it when it makes sense to do so.

If the team has the ear of the executive and the executive realizes his or her role and responsibility in assisting the team, the executive and team enter a clarification–negotiation process. Either the executive or the team, after they have adequate clarity, should be in a position to accept or modify the request (counter-proposal) until an agreement is reached. (Often the team's leader or manager negotiates with the executive on behalf of the team.) The whole team's understanding and agreement is still important to achieve. The agreement is a promise or set of promises to meet the negotiated terms. There are many promises given, some by the team or teams and some by the executive in support of the team. This latter may be discouraged by an organization's culture. In some organizations, it would be more acceptable for a team to fail to meet a commitment than to refuse or negotiate a request from an executive.

The team then performs the actions necessary to complete the commission. During this performance phase, the team is often off "doing its thing" and the executive is subjected to the surprising results, not having taken adequate time to monitor the progress of the team and/or not having arranged for the team to report progress adequately. The team "performs" and the executive wonders what went wrong! Or the team performs and wonders why the executive is unsatisfied with its work. The project is either declared completed (sometimes simply because the due date has passed and not because the work is finished) or the executive redirects the team. Too often, an adequate assessment is not conducted to determine why things went off track.

These failures of communication result in the executive feeling that his or her teams cannot perform or deliver results. In fact, there is no way for either the team or the executive to complete the commission.

It is critical that the launch of the initiative have clarity and be well-structured. It is important from the executive's standpoint to provide clarity and set expectations. As the executive, you must help the team to understand what you need, want, or desire.

The following can be used as a guide to assist the executive in creating a commission document, a sample of which is shown in Figure 2. The process is sponsor-driven and leads to a relationship and trust, while at the same time bringing about a result from the team that meets the needs of both the executive and the team.

CREATING A COMMISSION DOCUMENT

The executive (sponsor) and any key stakeholders initially develop the commission as a document. (See Figure 2.) The purpose is for the executive to capture clear thoughts about what he or she wants done and to define the specific needs to be met, outcomes to be achieved, and boundaries within which to work. This statement can be either global or narrowly focused in nature. As the sponsor spells out the commission, the responsibility for ensuring clarity rests jointly with the sponsor and the team. It is the team's responsibility to understand the intent of the commission and gain clarification from the executive on any issues that are unresolved in any way, just as it is the executive's responsibility to explain his or her wishes. If this is a new responsibility for the team, or a new approach for the organization, or if trust between workers and the executive has not been established, it is the responsibility of both the executive and the team to work through the process.

Let us explore the specifics of the commission document.

Commission Statement

The *commission statement* is a paragraph that declares *what* the team is supposed to do, that is, what the sponsor expects the team to accomplish. For example, the team may be commissioned to create an alternative work process that will make delivery of services more effective. The sponsor spells out his or her preliminary thoughts, and the team reacts to those thoughts by asking questions. This process helps the sponsor express and clarify what it is that he or she desires. The process begins with either the sponsor's or the team's (or its leader's)

Commission Statement

What the group is supposed to do—the desired outcome of the project

Deliverables

Product(s) due at the end or before completion of the commission. At a minimum always request:

- Project strategy
- Project work plan with a schedule
- Defined project products, for example:
  - Corporate needs analysis
  - List of organizational work processes and their production effectiveness rating
  - List of alternative work processes and their implementation costs

Success Measures

Objective measures used to tell if work and/or product is successful, for example:

- 10 percent increase in production
- 98 percent customer satisfaction rating
- Determining unnecessary company expenses leading to a 25 percent reduction in expense

Boundary Conditions

The limitations or rules that the group has to follow in the course of achieving their outcomes, for example:

- Project due dates
- Budget limitations
- How the product is supposed to look or be produced
- Project team composition

Figure 2. Sample Commission Document

invitation. This question-asking process clarifies the team's assignment and the sponsor's expectations.

Deliverables

The *deliverables* are the *products* to be created by the team. A team can generate several types of products. Examples include an evaluation and formal one-time report, an analysis of findings, or a determination of process performance measures. Additional deliverables—such as the sponsor requesting a review of the team's project approach strategy, project work plan, or timeline—are often overlooked. These specific deliverables can be captured utilizing a formal project management approach. This assists the sponsor in understanding the team's strategy and process to achieve the commission. The sponsor should make such communications a part of his or her request of the team. An initial agreement on deliverables and their timing reduces the team's risk of not fulfilling the sponsor's needs. A list of deliverables, including the actual products that the sponsor desires, ensures that the team is clear about what has been commissioned.

Success Measures

Success measures are what the sponsor will use to determine the success of the endeavor and the performance of the team. The sponsor can employ a series of measures to provide feedback to the team and also measure the effectiveness of the endeavor.

Different types of measures that individuals and organizations use have been explored elsewhere (Simon, 1998b). Measurement can be categorized as either hard or soft. *Hard measures* include such things as cost (contribution to the bottom line), quantitative output (measurable number of units output), and time. *Soft measures* include such things as customer product usability and team or individual practitioner performance measures. In any case, the measures should be meaningful to both parties and relate directly to the commission.

The sponsor must select types of measures that will reflect the desired outcomes. The selection of the measures helps to keep the team focused on what is important to the sponsor and organization and so creates a set of guidelines for the team.

Boundary Conditions

Boundary conditions include limitations or rules established by the sponsor with which the team needs to comply. The boundary conditions form the limit within which the team must function. For example, a product delivery date is a simple boundary condition. Other types of boundary conditions could include team composition (cross-functional team versus homogeneous team), the product's appearance (a handout or a slide presentation), and specific restrictions (jointly produced by union and management). Boundary conditions imposed by the legal, corporate, or external environments are also desirable to include, particularly if they are not common knowledge within the team (for example, compliance with OSHA requirements). Boundary conditions are not meant to be ways to micro-manage the team, but to define or limit how the work is accomplished.

DEVELOPMENT OF TEAM STRATEGY AND PLAN

After the dialogue has been completed between the sponsor and the team, the team determines how it will work internally and provides its plan to the sponsor. This plan creates expectations for the sponsor as well as creating the team's promise of delivery.

The sponsor must understand the team's concept of the project, the strategy the team will use to fulfill its understanding of the project, and the team's plan for fulfilling the project. In addition, it is important that the team make time to "check in" with the sponsor, to "check out" its undertaking. Figure 3 presents a sample team project summary and description form.

CONCLUSION

The disappointment caused by the failure of teams to perform is a manifestation of the failure of the executive to communicate clearly enough. If you, as a sponsor, want to get something, it is important that you take the time to say clearly what you want. Critical to the success of commissions is a conversation about the formative phase of a relationship—the agreements between the executive and the team—and what has to be done to structure the relationship to achieve what you want.

This self-design method presented here creates an environment for the executive, managers, and teams to meet each other's professional and personal needs, while at the same time contributing to the overall success of the organization. The executive and team must develop an effective and focused process that will lead to the desired results.

Formation of relationships between the executive and the team is critical to the success of any endeavor. Sponsors and teams must come to well-thought-out agreements in order to be successful. They must also strive to improve their working relationships to build better, stronger, and more fulfilling relationships that will in turn lead to higher performance and increased effectiveness.

Team Project Description	
Project Name:	Project Sponsor:
Projected Start Date: Projected End Date:	Team Leader:
Estimated Project Cost:	Team Members' Names:

Description of Project (team's understanding of the project):

Project Assumptions (team's understanding of why the project and the sponsors desire/need the project):

Figure 3. Team Project Description

Current Situation Assessment (need for the project):

Future State (desired outcome):

Team Strategy (how the team is going to achieve its results):

Project Goals	Project Objectives
Goal 1	Objective 1

Figure 3.   Team Project Description, *(continued)*

Project Goals	Project Objectives
	Objective 2
	Objective 3
Goal 2	Objective 1
	Objective 2
	Objective 3

Figure 3. Team Project Description, *(continued)*

References

Drucker, P. (1993). *Management: Tasks, responsibilities, practices.* New York: Harper and Row.

Flores, F. (1997). The leaders of the future. In P.J. Dunning & R.M. Metcalfe (Eds.), *Beyond calculation* (pp. 175–176). New York: Copernicus.

Katzenbach, J.R., & Smith, D.K. (1993). *The wisdom of teams: Creating the high-performance organization.* Boston, MA: Harvard Business School Press.

Kern, A.B. (1997). *Managing high performance learning teams.* Unpublished article. Ann Arbor, MI: Business Development Group.

Kotter, J.P. (1999). *On what leaders really do.* Boston, MA: Harvard Business School Press.

Simon, N.J. (1998a). The A^2D^4 process for designing and improving organizational processes. In *The 1998 annual: Volume 2, consulting.* San Francisco, CA: Jossey-Bass/Pfeiffer.

Simon, N.J. (1998b, July/September). Determining measures of success. *Competitive Intelligence, 1*(2).

Simon, N.J. (2000). Key stakeholder analysis: Preparing to introduce a new organizational idea. In *The 2000 annual: Volume 2, consulting.* San Francisco, CA: Jossey-Bass/Pfeiffer.

Neil J. Simon is the president of Business Development Group, Inc., based in Ann Arbor, Michigan. Mr. Simon has more than twenty-five years of experience in improving organizational and individual performance. He lectures and presents interactive workshops in areas relating to organizational culture, organization change, and organizational and individual performance. He has published numerous articles in business, clinical, and health care journals. Mr. Simon holds a master's degree in educational psychology from Eastern Michigan University and conducted his post-graduate studies at the Fielding Institute in Santa Barbara, California.

CONTRIBUTORS

Kristin J. Arnold
Quality Process Consultants, Inc.
48 West Queens Way
Hampton, VA 23669
   (757) 728–0191 or (800) 589–4733
   fax: (757) 728–0192
   e-mail: karnold@qpcteam.com

Andy Beaulieu
10713 Lady Slipper Terrace
North Bethesda, MD 20852
   (301) 231–0077
   e-mail: Andy_Beaulieu@erols.com

Robert Alan Black, Ph.D.
Cre8ng People, Places & Possibilities
P.O. Box 5805
Athens, GA 30604–5805
   (706) 353–3387
   e-mail: alan@cre8ng.com
   URL: www.cre8ng.com

Michael P. Bochenek, Ph.D.
Elmhurst College
190 Prospect Avenue
Elmhurst, IL 60126
   (630) 617–3119
   fax: (630) 617–6497
   e-mail: michaelb@elmhurst.edu

Patricia Boverie, Ph.D.
Associate Professor
OLIT EOB 105
University of New Mexico
Albuquerque, NM 87131
   (505) 277–2408
   fax: (505) 277–8360
   e-mail: pboverie@unm.edu

Brooke Broadbent
Vice President, Knowledge
   Management
Learneze.com
5939 Jeanne D'Arc Boulevard
Orleans, Ontario
Canada K1C 2S3
   (613) 837-6472
   fax: (613) 834-1874
   e-mail: brooke@learneze.com
    or brooke.broadbent@ottawa.com
   URL: www.learneze.com
    or www.e-learninghub.com

Richard L. Bunning, Ph.D.
Phoenix Associates (U.K.) Ltd.
57 Higher Lane
Rainford, Merseyside
WA11 8AY England
   44 (0) 1744 884430
   fax: 44 (0) 1744 882787
   e-mail: rbunning@dircon.co.uk
   URL: hxassoc.com

Marlene Caroselli, Ed.D.
Center for Professional Development
324 Latona Road, Suite 6B
Rochester, NY 14626–2714
   (716) 227–6512
   (800) 876–4090 (for book orders)
   fax: (716) 227–6191
   e-mail: mccpd@aol.com
   URL: http://hometown.aol.
    com/mccpd

Harriet Cohen
President
Training Solutions
P.O. Box 984
Agoura, CA 91376–0984
(818) 991–8116
fax: (818) 991–2007
e-mail: Tsolutions@prodigy.net

Shonn R. Colbrunn
MSX International
Visteon World Headquarters
5500 Auto Club Drive,
   Suite 1 West #378
Dearborn, MI 48126
(313) 317–4543
fax: (313) 390–9309
e-mail: scolbrun@visteon.com

Christina L. Collins
Phillips Associates
23440 Civic Center Way
Suite 100
Malibu, CA 90265
(310) 456–3532
fax: (310) 456–8744
e-mail: ccollins@phillips-
   associates.net

Melissa I. Figueiredo, M.S.
Department of Psychology
VCU Box 842018
Richmond, VA 23284
(804) 225–3866
e-mail: mfiguei@vcu.edu

Paul L. Garavaglia
57 Dennison Street
Oxford, MI 48371
(248) 969–4920
fax: (248) 969–2342
e-mail: ADDIEGroup@aol.com

W. Norman Gustafson
Sanger Unified School District
1705 Tenth Street
Sanger, CA 93657
(559) 875–7121
fax: (559) 875–8848
e-mail: WNGUS@HOTMAIL.COM

Edward Earl Hampton, Jr.
Performance Perspectives
2478 Danielle Drive
Oviedo, FL 32765
(407) 971–1060
fax: (407) 977–9194
e-mail: ehampton@mail.ucf.edu

Lois B. Hart, Ed.D.
President, Leadership Dynamics
10951 Isabelle Road
Lafayette, CO 80026
(303) 666–4046
fax: (303) 666–4074
e-mail: lhart@seqnet.net

Nancy Jackson
592 South Victor Way
Aurora, CO 80012
(303) 340–8518
e-mail: Nansolo@aol.com

Bonnie Jameson, M.S
1024 Underhills Road
Oakland, CA 94601
(510) 832–2597
fax: (510) 835–8669

Michelina (Micki) Juip
Hurley Medical Center
Diabetes Center
2700 Longway Boulevard, Suite F
Flint, MI 48506
(877) 877–1215
e-mail: mjuip@aol.com

J. Elaine Kiziah, M.S.
Department of Psychology
VCU Box 842018
Richmond, VA 23284
    (804) 225–3866
    e-mail: jekiziah@vcu.edu

Michael Kroth, Ph.D.
Senior Organizational Consultant
Public Service Company
    of New Mexico
M.S. 1001
Alvarado Square
Albuquerque, NM 87158
    (505) 241–2592
    fax: (505) 241–4314
    e-mail: mkroth@unm.edu

Robert William Lucas
President
Creative Presentation Resources, Inc.
P.O. Box 180487
Casselberry, FL 32718-0487
    (407) 695 5535
    fax: (407) 695-7447
    e-mail: cprbluca@magicnet.net

Debbie Newman, MA, MFCC
Working Relationships
16055 Ventura Boulevard, Suite 717
Encino, CA 91436
    (818) 385–0550
    fax: (818) 891–2926
    e-mail: WorkingRel@aol.com

Steven L. Phillips, Ph.D.
Phillips Associates
23440 Civic Center Way
Suite 100
Malibu, CA 90265
    (310) 456–3532
    fax: (310) 456–8744
    e-mail: sphillips@phillipsassociates.
    net

Kitty Preziosi
Corporate Catalyst
Preziosi Partners, Inc.
9441 Hollyhock Court
Fort Lauderdale, FL 33328
    (954) 915-0102
    fax: (954) 915-9912
    e-mail: KittyPrez@aol.com

Robert C. Preziosi
Professor of Management Education
Nova Southeastern University
School of Business and
    Entrepreneurship
3100 SW 9th Avenue
Fort Lauderdale, FL 33315
    (954) 262 5111
    fax: (954) 262-3965
    e-mail: preziosi@sbe.nova.edu

A. Carol Rusaw, Ed.D.
Associate Professor
Department of Communication
University of Louisiana, Lafayette
Lafayette, LA 70504
    (337) 482–6932
    e-mail: acr8632@louisiana.edu

Gary Schouborg, Ph.D.
Partner
Performance Consulting
1947 Everidge Court
Walnut Creek, CA 94596–2952
(510) 932–1982
fax: (510) 932–1982
e-mail: garyscho@att.net

Neil J. Simon
220 East Huron, Suite 250
Ann Arbor, MI 48104
(248) 552–0821
fax: (248) 552–1924
e-mail: njsimon@aol.com

Donald T. Simpson, Ed.D.
Don Simpson & Associates
Training and Organization
   Development
40 Mulberry Street
Rochester, NY 14620–2432
(716) 442–6501
fax: (716) 442–6501
e-mail: TrainOD@aol.com

Darlene M. Van Tiem, Ph.D.
University of Michigan, Dearborn
1310 Kensington Road
Grosse Pointe Park, MI 48230
(313) 593–3504
fax: (313) 884–8661
e-mail: dvt@umich.edu

Richard T. Whelan
Founder and Director
Chesney Row Consortium
   for Learning & Design
102 Adrossan Court
Deptford, NJ 08096
(856) 227–4273
fax: (856) 228–9036
e-mail: chesneyrow@aol.com

Susan B. Wilkes, Ph.D.
Department of Psychology
VCU Box 842018
Richmond, VA 23284
(804) 828–1191
e-mail: swilkes@saturn.vcu.edu

CONTENTS OF THE COMPANION VOLUME, THE 2001 ANNUAL: VOLUME 2, CONSULTING

---

*See Experiential Learning Activities Categories, p. 6, for an explanation of the numbering system.

**Topic is "cutting edge."